PORTRAIT OF BROTHER KLAUS

This design depicts The Divine Being (see inside page 52 and subsequently). To Brother Klaus, the centre represented the undivided Godhead and the three pointed ends entering the inner ring represent the Three Persons.

Engraving (date 1487)

Man of Two Worlds
Portrait of
BROTHER KLAUS

Saint Nicholas of Flüe
in Switzerland
1417 to 1487

by Christina Yates

William Sessions Limited
The Ebor Press, York
England

ISBN 1 85072 049 5

Printed in 9/10 Plantin Typeface
by William Sessions Limited
The Ebor Press, York,
England

Contents

Illustrations

CHRISTINA YATES WAS EDUCATED AT Sidcot, a Quaker co-educational Boarding School in Somerset, and in Geneva, where she worked from 1926 to 1927 at the Friends International Centre established during the early years of the League of Nations (now replaced by the United Nations). Later she was a housewife in Berlin during the first year of the Nazi regime (1933-4), and subsequently lived on a new housing estate in S.E. London, where she remained in touch with Quaker work in France, Switzerland and Germany and with local peace activities. After the second World War these varied experiences proved a useful preparation for 17 years (1953-70) teaching English to an international group of children at the Ecole d'Humanité in the Bernese Oberland. This was an offshoot from Paul Geheeb's Odenwaldschule which could not promote Paul Geheeb's educational principles under Hitler. It was while at the Ecole d'Humanité that Christina Yates first heard of Brother Klaus, and after her retirement spent several years studying the extensive literature in French and German about this extraordinary man who is famous in his native Switzerland but almost unknown in the English-speaking world. It is the aim of the present book to remedy this deficiency.

Acknowledgments

WE THANK THE FOLLOWING PUBLISHERS AND AUTHORS for permission to quote material detailed more fully in 'Sources of Quotations and References':

Staatskanzlei des Kantons Obwalden, 6060 Sarnen, Switzerland,
    for quotations from Robert Durrer's *Die ältesten Quellen*.

Patmos Verlag, Düsseldorf, Germany, and Professor Walter Nigg,
    for quotations from *Niklaus von Flüe: Berichte der Zeitgenossen*.

Kanisius Verlag, 1701 Freiburg, Switzerland, and Herr Werner Huber,
    for quotations from *Gespräch mit Bruder Klaus – der Pilgertraktat*.

Routledge & Kegan Paul
    for quotations from *C. G. Jung's Collected Works, Vol. II*.

Special thanks are due to Professor Guy Marchal of Basel University for advice on historical matters, but he is not responsible for any errors or omissions which may have occurred in the final draft.

The author is also grateful to Mrs. Rosa Aylward for much practical help, including supplying several illustrations, to Mrs. Barbara Clark and to many other friends.

Four illustrations (pp. 3, 14, 15, 31) by Tony Schneiders, Lindau.

This publication made possible with help from 'Pro Helvetia'.

Sources of Quotations and References

Explanatory Notes

The existence of bibliographical notes is not indicated by footnote numbers in the main text but the references can easily be picked up through the relevant page numbers given in Appendix III at the end of this book.

The chief sources used are from Dr. Robert Durrer's classic collection of the earliest sources, 'Bruder Klaus: die ältesten Quellen'. For full details see Appendix III.

A Commendation

Is IT REALLY POSSIBLE TO commend the life of a saint? And one as 'way out' as this 15th century Swiss family-man turned hermit and mystic?

The answer must be yes. Not because this or any other saint can ever be a perfect 'model' of Christian obedience, but because some lives are so rich in the gifts of the Spirit that even centuries later it is possible to share in the grace of these gifts and to be enriched by them.

Hagiography, the writing of the lives of the saints, should not be read less critically than any other kind of literature. It will convey different things to different people. Certainly the life – or the lives – of this Saint Nicholas provides more than enough food for thought to justify Christina Yates' carefully researched yet modest work: food for thought about a Christian whose fame spread because he had no need for the kind of food that sustains us mortals. Fasting is not much in fashion. This life inevitably raises important questions about its importance in the life of the Spirit. But for this, or any other age, it is as an apostle of peace that Brother Klaus is of far more than historical interest.

So, I warmly and gratefully commend this life of a very alternative and challenging 'Santa Claus'!

Paul Oestreicher
Director of International Ministry
Coventry Cathedral

Introduction

EVERY SWISS SCHOOLCHILD HAS HEARD of Brother Klaus, canonised in 1947 as Saint Nicholas of Flüe. In 1481 at the Diet of Stans his intervention saved the infant Confederation from civil war and probable disintegration. So far so good. But two further facts are usually added which tend to produce disapproval (or laughter) and disbelief. At the age of 50, having fathered 10 children, he left home and became a hermit. The natural reaction is to surmise, with Mark Twain, that he did so 'in order that he might reflect on pious themes without being disturbed by the joyous or other noises from the nursery.' If this thought arouses a tolerant smile or a cynical laugh, the second fact is equally troublesome. In his own lifetime he was revered and famous throughout Europe for a total fast which was believed to have lasted from the time he became a hermit until his death 20 years later. This combination of the reprehensible and the incredible effectively banishes Brother Klaus to a limbo of myth and superstition. Even the historical fact of his peace-making achievement at Stans, 'indisputably one of the most important turning-points in the history of [the] country' often loses focus in a haze of generalisations and even inaccuracies.

The enquirer who seeks beyond the brief paragraphs in the encyclopaedias and history books discovers a different picture of this remarkable man – human, very real and above all challenging. His personality has fascinated everyone who goes deeper into the story. The documentation is surprisingly plentiful, for soon after his death a collection was made of eyewitness accounts by a number of people who knew him well, including friends and neighbours since boyhood, two parish priests, and two of his sons; of his numerous visitors several recorded their impressions in journals and letters which have survived. One of the most valuable and detailed accounts was found in the travel-journal of Hans von Waldheim, a sensitive and observant visitor from north Germany. The 'narrative-visions' aroused the interest of the Swiss psychologist C. G. Jung and his colleague M.-L. von Franz.

The legend has become inaccurate in some matters and is probably embellished in others, but the core of well-attested fact is remarkable. Scholars would give a great deal to know half as much about Shakespeare. The phenomenon of the fast seems incredible but the evidence is unusually convincing. The question is considered in detail in chapter three and the reader must judge for himself.

Brother Klaus has been described as 'the forerunner of modern pacifism', but not all biographers would agree, and indeed pacifism as it is understood today did not exist in the late Middle Ages. Nor did Europe, nor did Switzerland. These concepts were undergoing rapid change in the turbulent 15th century. Joan of Arc, who symbolises the rise of a sense of nationality, died aged 19 when Brother Klaus was a boy of 14. Five years after his death Christopher Columbus discovered a continent (hitherto unknown to Europeans), and the idea of Europe acquired a new dimension. With the invention of the printing press and other technical improvements, books began to multiply; the first printed book about Brother Klaus appeared in Nuremburg, probably in 1487, the year of his death.

While the idea of the nation-state was becoming more concrete, even if national boundaries were still fluid, Christendom was on the eve of the great separation. When the split came, both sides, Catholic and Protestant, claimed Nicholas for their own and quoted him when it suited them. But Brother Klaus belongs to undivided Christendom.

Uncompromising he may have been, and hard on himself. But he was a reconciler, a positive force, a man of peace. Like George Fox, the Quaker, two centuries later, he 'lived in the life and power that takes away the occasion of all wars.'

The events of his inward and outward life still haunt those who overcome their first recoil. Who can understand the mind of a saint? Awe and humility hold one back. But the aim of a saint is not to have his mind understood. His aim is to follow the will of God. As he struggles and wrestles to do this, God becomes more real to those who encounter him – and this is the mark of a saint. Yet sometimes, as Klaus told a troubled youth who came to him for advice, seeking God is like going to a dance – 'Yes,' he repeated in his homely local dialect when he saw the young man's shocked expression, 'like going to a dance.' He also saw and barely survived a vision of the wrath of God. He has a message for our tormented age.

PART ONE

The Story

CHAPTER I

Life in Flüeli:
Family Man, Farmer and Citizen

THE BRÜNIG PASS IS CROSSED every year by thousands of foreign tourists travelling by road or rail between Lucerne and Interlaken but most of them are probably not aware that between Brünig and the Lake of Lucerne they are passing through the small Canton of Unterwalden, 'Brother Klaus country'. This region in the centre of Switzerland is the nucleus from which the modern Confederation developed. In the late 13th century representatives of what are now the Cantons of Unterwalden, Uri and Schwyz (which later gave its name to the whole country) met in a meadow overlooking the Lake of Lucerne and swore a perpetual alliance against their common foes. The event is still celebrated annually on 1st August with bonfires on the mountain tops and fireworks in the cities.

By stages during the 14th century the original three grew to eight. In the following century their fortunes became entangled with those of their powerful and power-hungry neighbours – the Kings of France and the Dukes of Burgundy to the west, the Habsburgs, usually dominating the Holy Roman Empire, to the north and east, to the south the Dukes of Milan and Savoy. The shifting alliances of these powers with each other and with the Confederates form the background to the story of Brother Klaus's life.

Small as it is, Unterwalden is divided into two 'half-cantons' : Nidwalden with its capital at Stans, and Obwalden whose capital is Sarnen. The tourist route runs through gentle, pastoral country, overlooked by sheltering hills. But at right angles to the main valley is a deep mysterious gorge, perhaps actually a rift caused by an earthquake, through which flows a mountain torrent, the Melchaa; just upstream from the gorge where the valley widens a little, is the place where Brother Klaus lived when he became a hermit – a few acres of grassy slopes and woodland known as The Ranft.

Nicholas von Flüe was born in 1417 near this wild Melchaa valley, in a hamlet overlooking the orchards that lead down to Lake Sarnen. His parents were farmers whose forefathers had been identified with the struggle for independence and who were themselves leaders in the local community. Klaus's mother came from the village of Wolfenschiessen near Engelberg, and Klaus remained in contact with this district throughout his life. This has some significance because a lasting impression must have been made on him by a hermit who lived there, Matthias Hattinger (or Huttinger), a 'Friend of God'. This was a lay movement practising a disciplined life of prayer and austerity. It is believed that many of Klaus's friends and advisers belonged to this movement, including Pastor Heini am Grund, who played an important part in his life. In 1467 when Klaus left home his original intention had been to join a community of the Friends of God in Strasbourg. At that time the Dominicans were among their leaders, and a Dominican friar left an important record of his conversation with Brother Klaus in The Ranft (p. 42).

The house where Klaus was born and the house where he later took his wife still stand in the hamlet of Flüeli above Sachseln. Later when he became a hermit, and received many high-ranking visitors, one of them (Albrecht von Bonstetten) described him as 'of low birth'; this was from the point of view of a nobleman unfamiliar with the social position of the more prosperous land-owning farmers in this district.

The chief sources of information about Klaus's early years come from the testimonies of two life-long friends and neighbours. The events were recalled long afterwards by two old men looking back, and inevitably their memories must have been coloured by the fact that even in his own lifetime he came to be regarded as a 'living saint' by many of his contemporaries, though it took nearly 500 years to have their verdict endorsed by Rome. They describe him as a pious and withdrawn lad and relate some strange experiences which he confided to them. From boyhood he found extra time for prayer, beyond the conventional times with family or in church and even as a child he practised a strict form of fasting. From evidence elsewhere of his warm-heartedness and kindliness (as an adult) one feels that perhaps his ordinary human qualities may have been taken for granted by those who knew him so well.

From the age of 16, Klaus became liable for military service and he took part in several campaigns, rising to the rank of captain. For 10 years from 1436 (when he was 19) there was civil war between Zürich on the one side and the remaining Confederates on the other.

A legend grew up that through his intervention the Convent of St. Katharinental (near Diessenhofen) was saved from pillage and destruction by troops from Unterwalden, but research into the movement of troops at the relevant time seems to disprove the story, although a crucifix supposed to have been used by the saint was preserved at the Convent as a sacred relic. Whatever the truth of the story it is significant that his two lifelong friends Erny Rohrer and Erny Anderhalden, testified after Klaus's death that 'even in war he did his enemies little injury, but drew aside and prayed and protected them as far as lay in his power.'

Some commentators seem to be baffled by these statements as somehow detracting from Klaus's courage and manhood. It will never be known just what was

Homestead of Niklaus and Dorothy

Niklaus and Dorothy (wooden sculpture)

meant by them but in view of the butchery and lawlessness shown by the victorious side in those days, it could simply mean that Klaus spared those who surrendered, did not join in the looting and tried to help any non-combatants who got caught up in the fighting. This is the interpretation of his first official biographer. He must have been shocked by the failure to observe the rules of warfare laid down by the Covenant of Sempach signed by the Confederates in 1393, and by the breaking of solemn agreements.

In a fictional reconstruction of his life the author imagines him protesting at the notorious massacre of the surrendering forces at Greifensee (1441) a deed which later 'lay heavily on the consciences of the Confederates.' Even if imaginary, this story, like the incident at St. Katharinental, is in harmony with the testimony of Klaus's two old friends.

In 15th century Unterwalden the right to vote on local affairs was acquired by males at the age of 14, and as soon as he was eligible, young Klaus was taken by his father to the meetings of the local council (*Landsgemeinde*). The lists of office-holders in Obwalden for the years 1442-1467 are missing, and exact details of Klaus's periods of office are not known, but he served as councillor and magistrate (probably immediately succeeding his father) and once, in 1462, he represented Obwalden at a meeting of the four 'Forest Cantons'[1] (the three original cantons plus Lucerne) in a dispute with the church. In another lawsuit with the church Klaus and his friend Erny Rohrer took a leading part in resisting the unjust demands of the absentee priest for a tithe of the local fruit harvest, though giving no service in return. This tax had the curious name of the 'wet tithe'. For many years there had been no resident priest in Sachseln and Klaus was baptised in the neighbouring church of Kerns. Later in his life, Oswald Isner, parish priest in Kerns, was his confessor and confidant.

Like other men of independent mind, Klaus appeared to be unimpressed by wealth or high rank, whether in others or as a possibility for himself, and in surviving records he often heads the list of deputations appointed by the village or commune to deal with some local dispute. The Swiss practice of rotating the more important offices (for instance to this day the presidency of the Swiss Confederation) already existed in Obwalden for appointment to the highest honour in the Canton, the office of *Landamman* (sheriff or chief magistrate). In due course Klaus would have succeeded to this office if he had not, by all accounts, 'strenuously resisted.' He became more and more disturbed by the dishonesty and corruption he encountered even among his fellow magistrates and finally he resigned. He told his family that he had seen flames issuing from the mouths of his fellow justices. This was believed literally by his contemporaries and at the least it is a memorable metaphor. Another record says that the final break came because he was unable to prevent an unjust judgment reached by bribery and other pressures. Perhaps this is why the relevant list of office-holders has disappeared.

In his late twenties, Klaus married a farmer's daughter, Dorothe (Dorothy) Wiss, who was probably not more than 16, perhaps even younger, at the time of their marriage in 1444. He took her to live in a house which he built himself a few hundred yards from his parents' home and there in the course of the next 23 years 10 children were born, five boys and five girls. Periods of absence from home while on military

---

[1] The word 'Canton' was not in general use until the 17th century. See Chapter IV.

5

service continued for at least the first two years after his marriage, and Hans, their first child, was not born until 1447; Nicholas, the youngest, 20 years later.

Alongside the ordinary routine of work on the farm, instructing his children, going to mass on Sundays, serving as councillor and magistrate, representing his community when required, Klaus was always aware of another dimension and other priorities. His daily work is referred to incidentally by his contemporaries, in their accounts of his spiritual life. His friend Erny Rohrer recalls how, when a group of young people returned from work in the fields (probably at an age when they were just helping the grown-ups) Klaus, even as a young boy, would slip away to some retired spot to pray; Klaus himself told of a vision in which a beautiful lily is devoured by his favourite horse; there is more than one account of how, when he and his son Hans were clearing brambles in the upper Melchaa valley, Klaus was attacked by the devil (as he believed) and was hurled over a boundary ridge (a drop between two levels, as is common on a steep alp) and lay unconscious till his son picked him up. Hans reported that when his father at last came to himself, still feeling very shaken, all he said was, 'Well in God's name that was a bad turn the Devil did me, but I suppose it was all according to God's will.'

As time went on, the awareness of these other realities and the conflict between the claims of his duties as family man and citizen on the one hand and something else he believed he was meant to do, became increasingly insistent. At the age of 16, he told his friend Erny Anderhalden many years later, he had had a vision of a beautiful high tower rising where the chapel and his hermitage now stand. It was because of this vision that from youth up he was inclined to seek solitude. Fritz Blanke in his study of Klaus's inner life discusses why it took him 35 years to decide to become a hermit, since he thinks Klaus knew that the tower symbolised a hermit's life. Certainly he appears to have had intimations from an early age, probably even before the vision at 16, that God had some special task for him. Heini am Grund, parish priest at Stans and previously at Kriens, near Lucerne, recorded that Klaus had told him a strange tale of pre-natal memories foreshadowing his destiny, which is dealt with in more detail in Part Three.

But for a man to be convinced that God has a special task for him, and to know precisely what it is, are not the same thing. Klaus could hardly have become a hermit at 16 years old, and he does not appear to have felt a call to become a priest or monk. The years of ordinary occupation were in fact the ideal preparation for his later life; hard physical work; a happy married life with a large, well-spaced family of boys and girls, the eldest grown up and married while the youngest was still a baby; involvement in all the problems and disputes of a vigorous and obstinate peasantry; travel beyond his native canton both as a soldier and (at least once) on a deputation to meet representatives of three other cantons. It is hard to imagine a better way of gaining the wisdom which enabled him to advise and help the crowds of people who visited him during the last 20 years of his life. At the same time he was deliberately preparing himself in other directions. The two Ernys and his son Hans all testify to his unusually strenuous fasting. (More details are given in Part Two, 'The Eyewitnesses'.) Hans also relates how his father would go to bed at the same time as the rest of the family but in the night would get up to go and pray near the stove in the living room; or he would even leave the house and go down to The Ranft in the night. Dorothy must sometimes have woken up to find him gone.

His visions and dreams will be described later in more detail, but there is one prayer which may serve here to illustrate the nature of the growing struggle in his mind. Unlike the strange picture reproduced in the first book about him (the Pilgrim's Tractate), or the long narrative visions, there is nothing mysterious or controversial about the prayer – it is just a straightforward challenge, as haunting today as when it was first offered. Although Klaus did not originate it, it has come to be known as 'Brother Klaus's Prayer'.

> O Lord, take Thou from me
> All that makes me turn from Thee.
> O Lord, give Thou to me
> All that draws me nearer Thee.
> O Lord, take myself from me.
> Give me all and whole to Thee.

This was the spirit in which he lived and the basis of all his search, and as time went on the inner conflict grew more intense. It became increasingly clear to him that to do his duty conscientiously in the place where he found himself was not enough.

In his mid-forties, he suffered a serious depression. Some years later he told a visiting friar that for two years 'he could find no peace by day or night but was brought so low that even my dear wife and the company of my children were a burden to me.' While he was in this state, his 'intimate and trusted friend' Heini am Grund, then parish priest at Kriens, came to see him. Am Grund may have heard of his friend's trouble and made a special visit, or perhaps Klaus or someone else sent for him, for Kriens, on the outskirts of Lucerne, is some distance from Flüeli. The priest advised all sorts of remedies, but Klaus said he had tried them all and they were no use. Then am Grund explained to him how to divide his meditation on the passion between the seven canonical hours. Klaus welcomed this suggestion and put it into practice at once, but 'because I was involved in many worldly affairs and official responsibilities I found . . . my meditation lacked concentration.' So he began to withdraw more and more frequently to The Ranft. It is possible that Father am Grund gave him a book with woodcuts illustrating the stages of the passion – such books were circulating at that time. This would have helped Klaus, who could not read, to memorise the subject of each meditation, and it would probably not have been long before he knew them by heart. This exercise, directing his thoughts away from himself at regular intervals throughout the day, steadied him and brought him to a point where his path became clear. A lifelong student of Brother Klaus, in an imaginative reconstruction, thinks that at some time during this period he must have consulted Heini am Grund about the insistent call to leave home, and received the advice that it could hardly be a call from God if he could not obtain his wife's agreement.

It was probably after the birth of young Nicholas that Dorothy finally consented to the parting. Tradition and such clues as can be gleaned from the records agree that the marriage was a happy one and that Klaus loved his wife. How far Dorothy understood his inner life is not known, but she can hardly have lived for so long by his side and not have been aware of its importance for him. For more than 20 years they shared a bedroom, a room you can still see in Flüeli, as also the stove in the living-room where he knelt to pray in the night and the door he left unlatched when he strode through the darkness to The Ranft.

There is no contemporary record of the discussions they had, but the earliest official biographer (Wölflin) claims to have used accounts from reliable witnesses.

He unfolded his plan to his beloved wife, who was also his trusted adviser: he had resolved to put the attractions of the world behind him and to seek out a suitable place where in solitude he could devote himself entirely to spiritual contemplation.

He took great pains to persuade her, since her agreement was necessary, but for a long time his efforts were in vain, because of all the domestic complications. On his side he remained convinced that his whole way of life at present was incompatible with his vow to renounce the world, so he continued to urge her in spite of her entreaties, and at last reluctantly she gave her consent.

CHAPTER II

The Break

THE SUMMER OF 1467 WAS AN eventful one for the family. On 24th June a son was born and was called Nicholas after his father. A few weeks later Hans, the eldest son, now 20, married Elsbeth von Einwil. In the early autumn Klaus took leave of his family and left home for good. In Wölflin's account one can sense Dorothy's pain behind the bare narrative. It is believed that the older sons did not really approve, but when their mother had once decided that Klaus's word was final – 'God will have it so' – she appears to have supported him loyally, upheld by the very love which made her fight so hard to keep him, and no doubt also because in her own less dramatic way she too was trying to do God's will. According to tradition she wove his cope herself.

So the date was fixed, 16th October 1467, St. Gallus's Day. St. Gallus was the Irish monk who more than 800 years earlier had left his home to preach the gospel in Switzerland.

Barefoot and bare-headed, wearing a coarse brown robe with a girdle of rope, Klaus took nothing with him but a staff and a rosary. There is a tradition that he intended to join the Friends of God, a community in Strasbourg. He set off at dawn and towards evening he was within sight of the little town of Liestal, between Lucerne and Basle. Here he was halted by an alarming sight – Liestal was lit up by a lurid red light, as if on fire. There seemed no point in seeking shelter there, so he turned aside and approached a farmhouse. In those days, when inns were few and far between, a prosperous farmer (as he had been up to now) would have had no hesitation in asking for food or drink at a strange farm – he would have offered similar hospitality to anyone knocking at his own door.

The farmer made no reference to the strange light over Liestal, which he did not appear to see, but questioned Klaus about his plans, and when he heard them he advised Klaus to return home, which he said would be more pleasing to God than becoming a burden to strangers, and anyway the Confederates were not always viewed with a kindly eye beyond their own borders. He offered hospitality for the night, but Klaus refused and sought a sheltered spot under a hedge.

There followed an experience even more crucial for Klaus's destiny than the decision to leave home. It seemed to him that God was telling him to return – if not to his farm and family, then at least to the district he came from. How far he was influenced by the farmer's advice, how far it merely confirmed his own growing doubts, is not known. From the way he later described the experience to Erny Rohrer and Heini am Grund, it seemed to come more as a bolt from the blue, a sort of Damascus Road. In a dream, a beam of light pierced his body like a knife. His earliest biographer adds it was as if a rope were pulling him home. It must have been a shattering experience. If his neighbours had thought him crazy before, they would now think him a fool. But he had spent so many years of his life trying to discern God's will that his judgment by this time had become surer. This dream meant he had to go back, so back he went. The dream had another strange consequence – from this time on he lost all desire for food.

He retraced his steps and reached the family farm at dead of night. He crept into his own hay-loft and slept for a few hours, but was gone before daybreak. According to one story, his sons later saw the signs that someone had slept in their hay and said 'Some tramp has been here overnight.' There is no contemporary record of this, but it seems perfectly possible.

Meanwhile Klaus climbed higher up the valley beyond his house and remained there for several days without food. Then he was discovered by some men hunting game, among them his brother Peter, who was appalled at his emaciated appearance and implored him not to starve himself to death. Not only his fasting but the stresses of the past few weeks may well have given him a gaunt and haggard appearance. Klaus sent a message to the parish priest at Kerns, Oswald Isner, asking him if possible to visit him. He told Isner that he had fasted for 11 days, and asked his advice, in confidence, whether he should begin eating again or continue the experiment. He said he had always longed to live without food and thus be more independent of 'the world'. Isner relates what followed:

> He [Isner] felt Brother Klaus's leg above and below the knees, on which there was very little flesh, for he was wasted away to the skin, his cheeks quite thin and his lips quite shrunken. But when he had satisfied himself that the basis and justification of his fast was truly his love of God, he advised him that since God had allowed him to hold out without food for eleven days, then as long as he could stand it without starving to death, he might try for still longer, which is what Brother Klaus did, and from then on for twenty and a half years till the end of his life persisted in taking no bodily food whether by eating or drinking.

This mysterious business of the fast is discussed in more detail later.

By now of course the news of his reappearance was common knowledge. The fictionalised accounts of the consternation and indignation of the two elder sons are very plausible. What Dorothy felt is not known, but it is surmised that, having once accepted the break, she now defended his inexplicable behaviour as loyally as she could. People flocked to his refuge in the bramble thickets above The Ranft, leaving him no peace. Obviously Klaus could not spend the winter in the open – at that altitude there would soon be several feet of snow.

Erny Rohrer, recalling the sequence of events more than 20 years later, when he was about 80 (he was 10 years older than Klaus) says Klaus:

> saw four bright lights in the sky which showed him the place where they should build him a dwelling and a chapel, which was done at his desire, according to the revelation he had received.

In fact it was not as simple as that. Klaus had already had several visions and dreams pointing to The Ranft and before he left home had frequently gone there to pray in the night. Why did he not go straight there if not when he first left home then at least after he was turned back by the vision near Liestal? In spite of the way his thoughts were centred on The Ranft, it was so near home – about 10 minutes' walk – that the idea of living there permanently must have seemed ludicrous. Time was needed to see things clearly. With hindsight we know that to be available for his destined role in the settlement at Stans he could not go too far away. On the other hand it was essential that the break with his old life should be complete and final. But once this break was established, for himself and his family and in the eyes of the neighbours, the psychological distance was established, and the physical distance became less important. He never again crossed the threshold of his former home.

CHAPTER III

Life in The Ranft

THE RANFT, ON HIS OWN LAND, was the place he had always been drawn to. Not only his critics but also his friends and loyal supporters were within visiting distance. When the nine-days-wonder died down, he could settle there and establish a new way of life accepted by everyone. So after an interval of readjustment he chose a site on the steep hillside above the rushing Melchaa and with the help of friends constructed a primitive shelter.

Within the next 18 months there were some unforeseen developments. The local people – Klaus's friends and neighbours in the canton – were divided in their reactions to the reports of his remarkable fast. Some had no difficulty in believing without question that this was a miraculous sign from God, others were doubtful and wondered if perhaps he was receiving food secretly, others simply thought that he was an imposter. To set all these doubts at rest, the local authorities arranged a strict watch on all the approaches to The Ranft and kept it up for a month with great severity until they were satisfied that no food was reaching him. One report says that the testimony of the witnesses was sworn on oath. When it was officially accepted that the fast was genuine, a more permanent dwelling was constructed with a chapel attached. The hermitage consisted of two small rooms, one above the other, the upper room being the one Brother Klaus usually occupied. The lower room contained a stove. In the wall adjoining the chapel there was a small window through which the hermit could look down on the congregation and take part in the service. The cost of construction was met from public funds and by some compulsory labour (or perhaps this tradition arose because the force of public opinion made it difficult to refuse to help). Klaus's first biographer records that the work was done in spite of opposition from some of Klaus's relations, who said that there should be more stringent proofs and a longer test period before hard-earned money and time were spent on the project. (One senses some family criticism behind those few words.)

After the chapel was built it remained for it to be consecrated and for this it was necessary to satisfy not only the local people but the more distant episcopal authorities over this matter of the fast. Bishop Hermann of Constance sent a trustworthy deputy, his suffragen, Bishop Thomas of Agathopolis, to look into the situation. A draft of his instructions has survived, in which after summarising the reports which had reached him, Bishop Hermann continues:

> according to the testimony of the apostles, the angels of darkness not infrequently transform themselves into angels of light and perform wonders that are not based on right foundations and should not be heeded . . .

12

Therefore we entrust to you, in your official capacity, as one in whom we have the greatest confidence, the task of informing yourself exactly and in detail about the above-named circumstances, by private investigation and diligent examination . . . [asking you] to let us know as soon as possible whatever you find out that . . . seems to you to be proven or probable, so that we can make use of it for the spiritual health of the faithful.

Given in our palace at Constance in the year etc. . . . under our episcopal seal which is attached to this letter.

In a memorable interview, Bishop Thomas asked Brother Klaus what was the virtue most pleasing to God, and when Brother Klaus replied 'Obedience', Thomas immediately produced the bread and wine he had specially brought for the purpose, broke the bread into three pieces and ordered Brother Klaus to eat it. Klaus did not want to disobey the Bishop's command, but he feared the difficulty of swallowing after such long abstinence and begged to be allowed to eat just one of the three pieces. He could only manage to swallow even this with a struggle and could hardly get down a small sip of wine. Much distressed, the Bishop declared that the test had fully satisfied him and explained that he had only insisted on it in obedience to the orders of his superior.

The same day, 27th April 1469, the chapel was consecrated, so it is assumed that Bishop Thomas must have reported favourably on the result of his mission, although no document has survived except the rough draft of the original instructions from his superior bishop. A year later the Church's approval was endorsed by a letter of perpetual indulgence signed by 16 cardinals in Rome, which was confirmed and amplified by Bishop Hermann of Constance, who also sent Brother Klaus a gift of money for a chaplaincy fund and two six-foot high bronze candlesticks for the chapel. The latter, however, Brother Klaus passed on to the parish church at Sachseln. Many years later they were melted down and made into eight smaller candlesticks. In the light of the constant difficulties with the parish priests of Sachseln, lasting throughout Brother Klaus's lifetime, this gift may well have been an example of his peace-making spirit. Perhaps he was anxious that his chapel, however much he loved it, should not outshine the parish church in the value and splendour of its ornaments.

The way must now have seemed clear for Brother Klaus to devote himself to a life of single-minded contemplation, but if that was what he had supposed God had intended for him, events were to prove otherwise. The crowds who had flocked to see him when he first returned home had of course long since had their curiosity satisfied and the local gossip had died down. But news of his remarkable fast was spreading all over Europe. In his own lifetime he became famous for something which in our day seems incredible, whereas the achievement for which he is now regarded as historically important is not even mentioned by the earliest biographers.

To find solitude from the crowds who still found their way to The Ranft – some as genuine pilgrims, some probably merely as sightseers – he had to set off at first light and climb higher up the Melchaa valley to a cave or overhanging cliff where he could spend the day undisturbed. This he often did; the visions that came to him are described in Part Three.

One of his earliest visitors a few months after the consecration of the chapel, was a Dominican friar to whom he made a 'confidential communication'. This friar

13

Cell (on left) and chapel in The Ranft

Interior of cell

asked him if it was true that hé lived without earthly food, and in response Brother Klaus, after exacting a promise that his answer would not be revealed during his lifetime, began by describing his life before he became a hermit and in particular the serious depression from which he had suffered for two years . . . At this point the manuscript suddenly breaks off.

Another of Brother Klaus's early visitors was an anonymous Pilgrim from south Germany who many years later published an account of his conversation with the hermit in a work known as the *Pilgrim's Tractate (Pilgertraktat)*. The two men discussed what they understood by the love of God, the immaculate conception, the prayer for daily bread, the significance of calamities like the plague. Brother Klaus showed the Pilgrim a diagram which he called his 'book'. This was a simple drawing of a wheel with six spokes. The elaborate pictures based on the wheel diagram, reproduced by the Pilgrim in the Tractate, became closely associated with Brother Klaus after his death. The Tractate does not include personal details about Brother Klaus to compare with those recorded by his later visitors, Hans von Waldheim or Albrecht von Bonstetten, but the sections are linked by brief allusions to Brother Klaus's warmth and courtesy which seem more than a mere literary device, since they agree so closely with what other visitors describe.

Geiler von Kaiserberg, who later became a famous preacher at Strasbourg, visited The Ranft in 1471 or 1472 when he was studying theology at the University of Basel. From references in two sermons preached about 30 years later (and subsequently published) it is evident that his encounter with Brother Klaus made a lasting impression on him, and through him influenced his circle of friends in Alsace, including Jacob Wimferling and Peter Schott, who visited The Ranft with his father in 1482.

Another celebrity on whom Brother Klaus made a lasting impression was the Dominican friar, Felix Fabri, author of a famous travel book and later Prior of the Monastery at Ulm. His father had been killed by the Swiss in a battle in 1443 when Fabri was five years old and this had left him with a permanent hatred of the Swiss, but in spite of this he made a visit to Brother Klaus in 1475 and referred to it 20 years later in the course of a dissertation on fasting.

Hans von Waldheim, a cultured landowner from north Germany, first heard of the hermit from a stall-holder at the Yearly Fair in Halle where he went to buy strings for his son's lute. A year later, returning from a pilgrimage to several shrines in France, he took the opportunity to visit Brother Klaus and also met his wife Dorothy and the boy Nicholas (now aged seven). His journal is not only the most detailed, but also the most interesting, contemporary account of Brother Klaus, free of the pious digressions and moralising which in most other early writers pad out the story and set Brother Klaus at a distance as a hardly human figure. It is the only known first-hand account of Dorothy and young Nicholas. The relevant extracts from von Waldheim's journal are given in Part Two.

Very different is the record of a visit four years later by Albrecht von Bonstetten. He was an aristocrat who, as the Dean of the Monastery of Einsiedeln, had many contacts with scholars, diplomats and royalty. The reports which reached him in his monastery made him decide to go and see for himself and he made the journey with an 'honourable company' just after Christmas in 1478. Although Dean of an important monastery, he and his friends seem to have been much more intimidated by their encounter than Hans von Waldheim, who brought an atmosphere of bonhomie and relaxed courtesy wherever he went, whether in conversation with the innkeeper who put him up for the night, or the little seven year old boy (to whom he gave a 'tip'), or with Brother Klaus himself. When the hermit greeted him, von Bonstetten says 'My hair stood on end and my voice failed me.' However, after overcoming his first alarm, he had a good look round and described all he saw in some detail.

Apparently something had happened to Brother Klaus since von Waldheim's visit. His biographer Wölflin relates that everyone was terror-struck at the sight of him. Klaus himself said that his awesome appearance was due to a vision of overwhelming majesty. He had seen an enormous blaze of light surrounding a human face which was so terrifying that it had 'shattered his heart'. It is not clear whether his awe-inspiring appearance lasted all his life. This vision and its relation to his other visions is discussed later. C. G. Jung was particularly interested in the way Brother Klaus coped with the experience.

The point has been reached where it is necessary to consider the puzzling question of Brother Klaus's extraordinary fast. (The technical term in Catholic theology is inedia.) Klaus's two friends, Erny Rohrer and Erny Anderhalden, and his eldest son, Hans, all testify that Klaus had begun to practise a strict form of fasting many years before he became a hermit. Erny Rohrer says 'when he was still quite a young boy', and his son Hans said that he fasted

> four days a week – on Monday, Wednesday, Saturday and Sunday and that throughout Lent he ate nothing but a small piece of bread once a day, or a few dried pears, otherwise nothing warm, or any other food.

He had evidently trained himself to do a day's work on this.

This was not of course the total fast referred to by so many of the visitors to The Ranft. According to general belief this lasted for nearly 20 years – from shortly after he left home in October 1467 until his death in March 1487. He was known in his own lifetime as 'the living saint'. In the 10 years from 1475, the fast, and its duration, were reported in chronicles or official records in the Palatinate, Austria, Gruyère and in his own district of Obwalden. Hans von Waldheim was told of it in Halle in 1473.

Alongside the testimony of other people there is Brother Klaus's own attitude. The contemporary accounts of his character and personality make it even harder to imagine that he would have acquiesced in a 20-years' fraud, than to believe in the apparent miracle. When directly questioned about his fast he avoided a direct answer as far as possible. To Hans von Waldheim he just said 'God knows', but he did add to this ambiguous reply a detailed account of the scene with Bishop Thomas. To an arrogant abbot who asked, 'Are you the one who boasts not to have eaten for so many years?' he replied, 'I have never said and I do not say, that I eat nothing.' He told the Dominican friar who visited him in 1469 that he had never revealed the answer to this 'difficult question to anyone except a pious priest from Lucerne' (Heini am Grund); under seal of secrecy he agreed to tell the friar, but the manuscript breaks off abruptly before reaching the critical point.

In spite of having told the Abbot of St. Stephan that he never said he ate nothing – presumably exasperated by his supercilious tone and the accusation of boasting – two witnesses report him as directly referring to his fast. Erny Anderhalden testified

17

that Klaus had told him more than once that God had granted him three great mercies among others namely,

> first that he obtained the agreement of his wife and children to his life as a hermit, secondly that he never had any wish, longing or temptation to return to his wife and children from this [hermit's] life and thirdly that he was able to live without bodily food or drink, as he [Anderhalden] firmly believed him to have done.

In his statement in the Churchbook, Oswald Isner, the Parish Priest of Kerns, recorded that:

> As Brother Klaus had perhaps been closer to him than to anyone else, and he had greatly wondered what kept him alive, he had often asked Brother Klaus and pressed him about it for a long time and once in his little house Klaus had told him in great confidence that when he was present at mass and the priest partook of the sacrament, he obtained a strength from this that enabled him to live without food or drink – otherwise he could not have borne it.

These accounts of direct conversations with Brother Klaus seem to confirm that he was reluctant to discuss the matter, probably because he did not wish to seem to be claiming any special sanctity. Most of the accounts mention that he took neither food nor drink. Presumably 'drink' in this context means anything other than water.

Later accounts slightly alter Father Isner's testimony that it was the sight of the priest partaking of the sacrament which gave Brother Klaus his strength, and state that it was the bread and wine which he himself took at the communion service that nourished him. According to Durrer this idea gained particular currency after the reformation, when the Catholic Church was stressing the miraculous element in the Eucharist.

In the light of all the evidence available, Durrer concludes: 'If a purely historical question had been under discussion it would hardly have occurred to anyone to doubt these specific witnesses.'

He means, of course, if the 'historical question' had not been a mind-boggling miracle. It was not accepted even in Brother Klaus's day without challenge and investigation by both the civil and the religious authorities. But it *was* accepted and is an important element in his life which cannot be left out of the picture and quietly ignored.

Brother Klaus was not destined to spend the rest of his life in The Ranft without neighbours. The first to arrive was a 'disciple' (Brother Klaus would have rejected the term) from south Germany, Brother Ulrich. He made his way to The Ranft on foot through 'forests and trackless mountains' and explained to Brother Klaus that he sought refuge for his soul from 'the world [where] everything was so evil, sad, repulsive, bestial, bloody, barbaric and devilish and where the whole human race was a shameless pestilential band.' He felt sure that Brother Klaus was unique among hermits in his 'gentleness, piety and honesty.'

> When Nicholas heard these words from Ulrich, he modestly begged him not to praise him in such excessive language as long as he lived, but to postpone judgment on the merits of his piety until after his death.

Such effusiveness was bad for them both, he said. Praise should only be given after dangers overcome. He should praise not Nicholas, who was still a voyager on this

18

earth, but the pilgrim who had reached harbour. The hermit's life would bring joy if followed with reverent love, until finally the hermit himself came to delight in his calling, enduring with obedience its pains and privations. In this conversation the contrast between the two men is striking. Brother Ulrich full of despair, disgusted with the human race, Brother Klaus who undoubtedly knew just as much of human sin and sorrow, not dwelling overmuch on moral judgments but emphasising rather the joy to be found in a life of contemplation and self-discipline. But Klaus recognised the sincerity and seriousness of Brother Ulrich's vocation and by the time of von Waldheim's visit he was already established higher up the river on the opposite bank of the Melchaa. Although only an 'arrow shot' from The Ranft, this place had a different name – Mösli – as is still customary in rural areas, where each field however small has its own identity. Ulrich's simple house or 'cell' contained some books and religious pictures. He was an educated man who could read and write and no doubt he read and discussed the gospels with Brother Klaus and helped him with his correspondence.

Brother Ulrich would have liked to emulate Klaus's total fast, but he was no longer young. Wölflin's account of how Brother Klaus dealt with the problem illustrates his tact as well as throwing an interesting sidelight on his relationship with his wife:

He [Ulrich] managed with the help of Brother Klaus's prayers, to spend thirteen days in contemplation without food or drink and was troubled neither by hunger nor thirst. Then Brother Klaus broke a loaf of bread, which he had obtained for this purpose, into halves, handed him one and told him to dip it in the Melchaa river . . . and then eat it. He obeyed at once, took the piece of bread he had been offered and ate it as ordered, but unwillingly, for he had overcome his desire for food. But the next day, when the same thing happened with the other half, he was seized with such hunger that he could hardly believe it would ever be possible to eat enough to satisfy it. Nicholas had foreseen this and meanwhile had arranged for his wife to bring sufficient food. When he had eaten his fill, Brother Ulrich asked the Friend of God why he had not allowed him to persist any longer in his fast. He received the answer that this experiment was enough, for that was the way God willed it.

From this time on, according to reports, Brother Ulrich daily ate only three small pieces of bread dipped in water. Later a chapel was built near his dwelling which is still there today. He survived Brother Klaus and is buried in Kerns.

CHAPTER IV

The Covenant of Stans

The Covenant of Stans was 'indisputably one of the the most
important turning points in the history of our country.'

(A. P. Segesser, 1879)

BROTHER KLAUS HAS EARNED A permanent place in the history of Switzerland for
his peace-making role during the internal conflicts that followed the Burgundy War
(1475-77) and were settled by the Covenant of Stans in 1481. To assess the
importance of his contribution some knowledge is needed of the situation in the
years preceding the settlement.

Present day Switzerland is so well-organised and, in spite of some anomalies, its
frontiers are now so well established that it is difficult to imagine the situation as it
existed in the 15th century. It is also difficult to describe it with accuracy, for lack of
an appropriate vocabulary. There was no 'Switzerland'; 'Swiss' did not mean the
same then as it means now; the word 'canton' was not used. Above all, the events we
now see as landmarks only became recognisable as such with hindsight. They were
not signposts pre-existing to guide the 15th century policy-makers along a clearly
discernable road to the federal constitution of neutral Switzerland as it emerged in
the 19th century.

By mid-14th century the three original 'cantons' – Uri, Schwyz and
Unterwalden – had been joined by five more: Lucerne, Zurich, Glarus, Zug and
Berne. They called themselves simply 'places' (Orte) but for clarity the
anachronistic word 'canton' will be used in what follows. Within a few years the
eight had signed two agreements which mark the beginning of a common legislation
for the embryo Confederation. The first, the 'Pastors' Ordinance' (1370) regulated
the relationship between church and secular authorities and also contained clauses
safeguarding traffic, particularly on the St. Gotthard route. The second, the
Covenant of Sempach (1393), attempted to reduce the butchery and chaos inherent
in warfare by protecting non-combatants and establishing minimum standards of
military discipline.

There were also regional pacts between adjacent 'cantons' in various groupings
which formed an overlapping network. A further network of arrangements, some
temporary, some quasi-permanent, bound one or more individual cantons to their
immediate neighbours beyond the 'old' Confederation. Certain close allies came into
a special category called 'related places' (Zugewandte Orte). At the other end of the

20

scale, some regions had been seized by conquest from previous overlords and were jointly administered by the eight, working in pairs on a rota; the need for the whole parliament (Diet) to meet regularly to receive and discuss reports on these 'bailiwicks' fostered the development of a sense of unity and common interests between the Confederates.

But there were forces working in the opposite direction. The three original cantons were predominantly rural. Their economy was based on small farms worked by their owners. As early as the 15th century, a new pattern of agriculture, including the raising of cattle, was establishing itself; families were often large, and the available land could not employ, or keep, all its members on what is only modestly fertile land in difficult mountainous country. Many young men offered themselves to the highest bidder among foreign kings and other princes and would be paid for their services in war.

By contrast to these rural cantons the city-states – Berne, Zurich, Lucerne – had a different economic basis. Their wealth was created by commerce and by craftsmen organised in powerful guilds. Zug, lying between Zurich and Schwyz, had a foot in each camp, but on the whole was regarded as belonging to the rural cantons. Conflict of interests between rural and urban communities is a perennial problem, not peculiar to Switzerland in the Middle Ages, but in this case the polarisation between the two groups threatened the survival of the Confederation. Although the rural communities were less powerful in terms of wealth and population, the stamina and valour of their soldiers made them coveted allies. It was however the city states who assumed the role of leaders, often without due regard for the susceptibilities of the three original founders of the Confederation. This was bound to lead to conflict. It must be stated however that the sources of conflict were not simply economic. The form of government and the source of authority were different in the mountainous rural cantons. There was no aristocracy in the latter, in the sense in which this term was understood by men like von Bonstetten; the leaders of the community were independent farmers, whose forefathers had fought to free themselves from outside domination. Decisions were made in open-air meetings (*Landsgemeinde*). There was less concentration of power in a few hands, less scope for decisions behind closed doors.

On the other hand, in rural areas belonging to the cities, country folk were little better than serfs. When they rebelled, the rural cantons secretly or even openly sympathised with them. One of the most serious of these rebellions was in a valley south of Lucerne – the Entlebuch – where in 1478 there was a movement to break loose from the city. The leader, Peter Amstalden, negotiated secretly with agents from neighbouring Obwalden, where he had friends and kinsmen, but the plot was discovered, Amstalden was arrested, imprisoned in the grim Water Tower on the bridge over the Reuss in Lucerne, tortured and executed. This was a particular cause of tension between Lucerne and Unterwalden during the critical period following the Burgundy War.

The central cantons were also in a different position from the others in relation to foreign policy. Though renowned for their martial prowess, they could not expand their territory, except in the 'Ennetberg', the old Swiss word for 'beyond the mountain', that is, Tessin, beyond the Gotthard massif. For all their love of freedom for themselves, Uri and Unterwalden appeared to have had no scruples in conquering the territory on the far side of the Gotthard in order to protect their trade route and their southern frontier. But elsewhere they were hemmed in by fellow-members of the Confederation. The latter, on the other hand, felt themselves threatened from beyond their borders. They pursued a policy of expansion and foreign alliances, according to circumstances. Berne, for instance, particularly needed the support of Freiburg and Solothurn. In addition, her friendly relations with Savoy were a source of mistrust among other Confederates. Contrariwise in certain questions, Berne tended to side with the rural cantons against Lucerne.

In the second half of the 15th century the Confederates, in alliance with King Louis XI of France, defeated Charles the Bold of Burgundy in his ambitious attempt to set up a sort of buffer state or Middle Kingdom between France and the Holy Roman Empire. Charles the Bold was killed in 1477 at the Battle of Nancy, and the enormous treasure which he took with him on his campaigns – articles in gold and silver and precious jewellery – was captured by the Swiss. The frugal hardworking farmers of the Forest Cantons became aware of luxuries and wealth hitherto beyond their imagining, but their military prowess was not matched by the diplomatic skills needed to hold the fruits of their victories.

In the spring of 1477 a group of disgruntled ex-soldiers from the three original Forest Cantons decided to take the law into their own hands and set off to collect money promised them by Geneva after the 1475 campaign in Vaud. Gathering forces as they went, they marched behind a banner bearing a sow, and called themselves the 'Company of the Mad Life' – today they might have said 'Crazy Gang'. Looting and pillaging as they went, their numbers had increased to 1,800 by the time they reached Freiburg. Here they were halted by gifts of wine and cash and the promise of a final settlement with Geneva, which was achieved in 1478 with the help of Berne. This breakdown of law and order in an intercantonal 'invasion' seriously alarmed the city-states, and in May 1477 Berne, Zurich and Lucerne signed an agreement (*Ewiges Burgrecht*) with Freiburg and Solothurn which in effect took precedence over the agreements or pacts already existing between the three cities and the five rural cantons. This particularly embittered the relationship between Lucerne and the three other Forest Cantons. All the latter felt threatened when their influential neighbour joined up with four other cities, two of them non-members of the Confederation. Hitherto their majority (five rural cantons, three cities) had compensated for their inferiority in resources and population. There was a strong desire on the part of the city states for more centralised authority and for inter-cantonal arrangements to control rebellious subjects. The rural cantons on the other hand were in favour of as much independence as possible and wanted to retain the influence they had hitherto enjoyed.

This was the complicated background to the long-standing difficulties solved by the Covenant of Stans. The widespread belief that it was simply a dispute over the division of the Burgundian booty is incorrect. The root of the trouble was not one single issue but the whole relationship between the members of the Confederation, which was full of confusions and contradictions, with inadequate machinery for dealing with them. 'There was hardly enough cohesiveness . . . to permit the use of the term Confederation.' (William Lloyd.)

The points of interest in relation to Brother Klaus are: What exactly was settled at Stans? To what extent and in what way did Brother Klaus contribute to the final agreement?

22

The *legend*, still widely believed, runs as follows: after a stormy meeting in the Town Hall negotiations were broken off and the deputies planned to return home to report deadlock. Civil war seemed inevitable. At the eleventh hour Brother Klaus appeared in person and by a dramatic appeal persuaded them to think again. As a result a peace formula was miraculously agreed and war was averted. This version became so widely accepted that a 17th century mural over the entrance to the Memorial Church at Sachseln shows Brother Klaus in the Town Hall at Stans, addressing the assembled deputies.

The real facts are different but in their way no less remarkable. Brother Klaus was not present in person at Stans – he simply sent a message by his friend Heini am Grund. The 'peace formula' was not some hastily composed document miraculously produced, but was almost identical with a draft that had been previously discussed. There is however universal agreement that it was Brother Klaus's intervention on 22nd December 1481 that saved the Confederation. This is clear from the letters of thanks and gifts sent to him after the settlement, from accounts by people present at Stans and of course from the tradition. It was the very strength of this tradition that created and fostered the belief in his physical presence at the deliberations.

But what exactly did Brother Klaus do or say? To identify his contribution required some detective work, and this was undertaken by Robert Durrer early in the 20th century. To understand the significance of the 'clues' he found, it is necessary to follow the stages of the negotiations which finally led to the Covenant of Stans. These continued, with interruptions, for several years. In the end two documents were ratified: firstly the agreement or 'Covenant' between the eight 'old places' and secondly a separate agreement *(Bundesbrief)* between the eight 'places' and the city-states of Freiburg and Solothurn. There were no less than six drafts of each of these documents before the final versions were arrived at, the first dated March 1478 and the last November 1481.

One of the major stumbling blocks was the *Burgrecht* agreement (see p. 22, 71) between Lucerne and the four cities, Berne and Zürich (within the Confederation) and Freiburg and Solothurn (outside it). Alongside numerous meetings of the full Diet, there were also separate efforts on the part of the rural cantons to detach Lucerne from its alliance with the cities. Every possible method was tried – legal proceedings, arbitration and friendly mediation – but all to no avail. In 1478 there was a lull in the internal disagreements while the Confederates attacked the Duke of Milan and became involved in complications with foreign enemies and would-be allies. Meetings of the Diet were fully occupied, says Durrer, 'with overtures of friendship from the King of France and his enemies; the heir to the Burgundy Kingdom, Maximilian; the Emperor himself [i.e. of the Holy Roman Empire] and his enemy Mattias Corvinus, the Pope; the Bishops of Strasbourg; and the Duke of Württemberg.' This list is a striking illustration of the complex situation the Confederates found themselves in and of their urgent need for internal cohesion in face of such external pressures.

Soon after the end of the war with Milan the rual cantons again attacked the *Burgrecht* agreement. Lucerne was their particular target because they maintained that her alliance with the other cities was incompatible with the alliance of 1332 with the three original Forest States (the alliance by which Lucerne became the fourth Forest State).

When this attempt failed there was a further lull of a year, until November 1480, when the rural cantons combined to attempt once again to detach Lucerne from the alliance with the city states. Lucerne refused, but offered to submit the dispute to arbitration. Now the difficulties assumed a new form. The Forest Cantons insisted on an equal number of representatives for each canton, which of course ensured a majority of three to one in their favour, whereas Lucerne demanded equal representation in the sense of the right to appoint as many arbiters as the three other cantons together.

It was in connection with the prolonged efforts to settle the dispute between the Forest Cantons that Brother Klaus first comes into the picture. The first 'clues' (as Durrer calls them) are found in 15th century account books in the Lucerne city archives recording payments made early in 1478:

On Saturday after the twelfth day [9th January]
Item lj lib.viij hlf Tanman to Brother Claus.

This payment to Peter Tanmann, a man of some consequence in Lucerne, was for expenses when visiting Brother Klaus. Two further payments were made, to Peter Tanmann and Peter von Meggen, during January and February. Durrer links the dates of these missions to The Ranft with the Diets and other negotiations over the *Burgrecht* dispute during the winter 1477-8.

According to the account books, similar payments were made in 1481 – a visit from Justice Feer and a companion in March; the gift of a cope to Brother Klaus in July and in mid-December 40 guilders for a perpetual mass. There are no direct records of what took place during these consultations, but there seems little doubt that Brother Klaus had been kept informed about the situation over a period of years and that from his forest hermitage he influenced the thinking of the men who produced the series of drafts which preceded the final documents. Presumably the purpose of the visits from Lucerne was not simply to seek advice, but also to ask Brother Klaus to discuss the problem with his fellow countrymen in Unterwalden. There must have been other visits and consultations of which no records survive.

The Diet of Stans was not merely about the *Burgrecht* problem. There was the dispute over the division of the Burgundy booty, and also – probably most important of all – the question of law and order, which had triggered off the whole dispute. The city states were determined to ensure that no more 'crazy gangs' or rebellious subjects should receive encouragement and asylum from sympathisers in adjacent cantons. For this reason they wanted a more powerful federal structure, which the rural cantons mistrusted. Brother Klaus, himself a man of some standing in the rural cantons, was in a strong position to urge compromise over this. In fact the final settlement laid down that rebels in one canton should not receive aid and comfort from a neighbouring canton.

The difficulty about admitting the two new members of the Confederation was overcome by putting them on a slightly different footing – as defined in the two separate documents – but in practice this was usually ignored. The two new cantons gradually slid into a position of equality but were not actually accepted by the rural cantons as more than close allies until 1501. The limitation on their right to fight separate battles and make separate treaties with 'outsiders' was a small price for them to pay for the closer relationship with other Confederates.

The more authoritarian federal structure desired by the city states was not achieved, but a way had been found to admit the two new cantons in spite of the opposition of the rural cantons. Thus concessions were made on both sides.

A formula was found to settle the dispute over the division of the Burgundy booty.

It was agreed that the Covenant of Sempach should be reaffirmed by oath at every meeting of the Diet.

The only eyewitness account of the events on 22nd December is by Diebold Schilling, who accompanied his father, the official scribe who actually penned the final agreement. Young Diebold was 21 at the time, and his account was written more than 25 years later in the course of his 'Luzern Chronicle', a general history of the period. It was Heini am Grund, he said, who realised the seriousness of the situation and had the idea of again appealing to Brother Klaus for help. He hurried on foot from Stans to The Ranft, a distance of 10 miles through the dark and cold of a midwinter night. He returned the following morning 'drenched in sweat', and with tears in his eyes begged the deputies to assemble again 'for the sake of God and Brother Klaus' to hear the hermit's views and advice. Brother Klaus had forbidden Father am Grund to reveal the message except to the deputies assembled together in the Town Hall, no doubt to ensure that they did all assemble in one place as rapidly as possible without forming parties outside the Hall before the meeting began.

What the message actually was is not known. Schilling does not say, and no other records have come to light. There is very little difference between the agreements drawn up at the November Diet and the documents signed in December. But the dramatic change in atmosphere affected not only the urgent question of signing the two documents but also the sorting out of loose ends not formally dealt with on that day. Although the Covenant was a compromise, and left some points unsettled, it provided a basis for the development of the Confederation for more than 300 years. It worked because of the determination of all concerned to make it work, and their confidence that the points left outstanding could be settled piecemeal on a basis of mutual trust.

How far Brother Klaus's influence was due to his practical advice during the preliminary discussions and how far to the weight of his spiritual authority at the time of the final crisis it is no longer possible to determine. Probably the two factors interacted from the beginning. All accounts agree that it was his last-minute intervention that saved the Confederation at the critical moment. However important his counsels may have been during the years of rumbling disagreement, a clear lead at the moment of deadlock, from a man of great spiritual authority, was seized upon with eagerness. In spite of the friction, there was probably a strong undercurrent among the deputies of an ardent desire for peace.

A leading figure in the final stages of the negotiations was the Town Clerk of Solothurn, Hans vom Stall, who took the responsibility of exceeding his formal instructions at the final Diet in December. The deputy from Freiburg felt unable to act without further instructions, but the Diet undertook to accept a retrospective signature and to accompany him back to his masters to explain the reasons for signing. This was successfully accomplished in the New Year.

The role of Heini am Grund was also crucial. Providentially he had become parish priest at Stans in the previous June. His previous parish had been the village of Kriens on the outskirts of Lucerne, his home town. As a close friend and confident of Brother Klaus he may well have discussed political matters with him, in particular the point of view of Lucerne, in addition to advising him spiritually, which we know he did from the records. In 1981 the route he took through the snow on that winter night 500 years earlier was made into a pedestrian pilgrim's way and a memorial stone was unveiled in Stans to mark the starting point.

A number of letters have survived describing the rejoicing which followed the settlement and expressing the gratitude which everyone felt towards Brother Klaus. The Mayor and Council of Solothurn sent a letter of thanks and a book to Heini am Grund and enclosed 20 guilders to be passed on to Brother Klaus for a perpetual mass for a year. To Brother Klaus himself they wrote:

> We have been informed that by the grace of God and his dear Mother you have achieved peace, quiet and concord by your faithful counsel and guidance. And that you spoke so much good on our behalf that we are now joined in brotherhood and a permanent union with the whole Confederation. For that we can fairly give great praise and thanks to the true God and the whole heavenly host and to you as a lover of peace . . .

Hans vom Stall wrote personally to Solothurn's allies, the Council of Mulhausen:

> Brother Klaus has wrought well and I managed well too. There is great rejoicing in the whole country with bellringing and singing to celebrate the achievement of unity. It may well be that you also will like to make a public announcement and praise God with bellringing and singing because of the united agreement that has been arrived at for the whole Confederation . . .

The representatives of the Council of Schwyz wrote in similar vein to their neighbours the Mayor and Council of Rapperswil:

> Everyone rejoiced to honour God and Brother Klaus as well, who had worked so hard and earnestly.

In May when the outstanding formalities with Freiburg had been completed the Town Council sent a handsome gift to Brother Klaus and his companion Brother Ulrich – two valuable lengths of material, one white and one grey, from their famous cloth factory.

CHAPTER V

Other Political Activities

BROTHER KLAUS'S INFLUENCE AS A political adviser was not limited to his decisive role in the constitutional crisis. His advice was frequently sought, particularly in 'international' matters, to use a somewhat anachronistic term. He could think objectively and see beyond narrow local interests. This did not necessarily increase his prestige in his home territory. It would be interesting to know the sources of his knowledge of the complicated political background both internal and external. Since he could not read it must have come through his many visitors. Any letters he received would have to be read to him. No doubt he had a shrewd idea of the trustworthiness or otherwise of his informants and could question them about points he did not understand, discuss the issues with some well-informed friend like Heini am Grund and think them over in solitude. Perhaps the very fact that he was not assaulted by all kinds of sophisticated media (as we are today) enabled him to see general principles more clearly. He had no vested interests and this was somehow dramatically symbolised by his fast and his renunciation of home and family.

During the years 1480-83 his visitors included messengers from the Habsburg Archduke Sigmund of Austria, who brought a gift of 100 guilders for the chapel; the secretary of two Italian counts with a letter of introduction from the authorities in Berne; and a special envoy from the Duke of Milan. A visit to The Ranft from high-ranking officials apparently seemed worth the trouble, to make sure that the hermit understood a particular point of view and could interpret it to his fellow countrymen in Unterwalden. Such contacts had begun even before the achievement at Stans. For instance, although Archduke Sigmund of Austria was a religious enthusiast with a particular penchant for the miraculous, there may well have been a further motive behind his valuable gifts – a gold chalice in 1474 as well as the 100 guilders in January 1481. To enlist their support in his manoeuvres against the King of France he was anxious to overcome the hostility of the people of Unterwalden towards their traditional Habsburg enemies.

The earliest known letter from Brother Klaus was to Archduke Sigmund thanking him for the 100 guilders brought by two officials from Chur. It was presumably dictated to Landamman Nicholas von Einwil (father-in-law of his son Hans) from whom he borrowed a seal.

A year later he acquired a seal of his own which was probably first used when the City of Constance appealed to him for help in their long-standing dispute with the Confederation. The problem arose from an unsatisfactory situation in the Bailiwick of Thurgau (not then an independent canton). It was administered by seven of the

27

eight members of the Confederation, but some rights were still in the hands of the City of Constance and this dual jurisdiction led to perpetual conflict and the risk of actual war. Various compromises had been suggested and rejected by one side or the other but in the atmosphere of general reconciliation after the December Diet a renewed attempt was made to settle the matter amicably. Berne (the canton not involved in the dispute) undertook to act as mediator. It was at this point that Constance wrote to Brother Klaus, an appeal which, as Durrer remarks, showed his growing political influence. Two meetings in February failed to settle the affair, but Constance remained faithful to the hermit's advice to pursue strictly legal channels and not to threaten military measures. At last after a further year of unsuccessful negotiations, in January 1483 agreement was reached through the mediation of the Bishop of Constance, Otto Von Sonnenberg.

Brother Klaus's letter is preserved in the Rosgarten Museum in Constance and is characteristic of his attitude to this type of dispute. The seal (that is, the wax impression) to which he refers is missing on the document but the silver seal itself is in the Convent of Thyrnan in Bavaria.

To the Mayor and Council of Constance:

> Greetings in the name of Jesus. I wish you every good thing and would not wish to achieve a good result in which you had no share. I understand what you have written. I also fully understand the request in your letter to pray to God on your behalf. I will do this in all sincerity, in everything however may God's will be done. For my part I will most willingly do what I can so that my words may bring peace but if it cannot be settled by mediation then let the law be strictly applied. In confirmation I have affixed my own seal at the end of this letter. God be with you.

> Given on the Wednesday before St. Blasius Day [30th January] in the year of our Lord 1482.

> Brother Klaus von Flüe

Brother Klaus's intervention was also sought in the affair of the Convent of Klingental in Klein-Basel, on the right bank of the Rhine, which started as a matter of religious discipline and ended in a serious political dispute. This Convent, like many others in the Middle Ages, was in effect a 'Home' for aristocratic single ladies, more or less the 15th century equivalent of a residential hotel; the ladies wore their own clothes and did what they liked to such an extent that the Convent was getting a bad name. The 'nuns' were evicted and some other ladies with a stricter discipline were installed. Both parties had supporters, and among those involved, apart from the Dominican Monastery, were the City of Basel, the Pope and Archduke Sigmund. Brother Klaus was asked by the Dominicans to intervene with the Archduke on behalf of the evicted ladies. It is believed that he refused and recommended leaving the problem to the Confederation to deal with. In the end the nuns who had been evicted offered the Archduke a bigger bribe than the nuns in occupation (8000 florins against 3-4000) and were reinstated. In view of the tortuous nature of the affair and the date of the appeal to Brother Klaus (January 1482, when the flurry of activity surrounding the settlement at Stans had barely died down) it is not surprising that he was reluctant to get mixed up in it.

The Covenant of Stans had united the Confederates in the most burning internal questions, but the individual cantons retained considerable freedom of action in their foreign policies. In 1482-3 the Cantons of Uri, Schweiz and Unterwalden, together with Zug, were involved in a prolonged dispute with the Duke of Milan in which the other Confederates, especially Lucerne, tried to mediate. The main point at issue was an agreement exempting Swiss traders from local customs duties in six specifically named towns along the route between Switzerland and Milan. When the agreement came up for renewal the cantons particularly affected wanted to extend the exemptions to places 'named and unnamed' in the region. The Milanese refused. There was also disagreement about sums owing the Duke from the Confederation. The ducal agent Gabriel Morisini, who had arrived in Lucerne in the autumn of 1482, was reinforced the following spring by a special envoy, Bernardino Imperiali. In May the latter reported to the Duke that soldiers returning from foreign service were spoiling for a fight 'like hungry dogs'. At the same time agents from Venice were stirring up the already discontented ex-servicemen in the hope that they would attack Milan in the rear. Documents and emissaries travelled back and forth.

In June the Diet in Baden sent an ultimatum to Milan insisting on retaining the offending words 'named and unnamed' and fixing a deadline – St. Ulrich's Day (4th July) for their acceptance. Secretly the deputies at Baden decided that they would not make war over these two words, but meanwhile the war fever had reached a dangerous level, particularly in Unterwalden, and Imperiali had enlisted the help of an influential merchant and councillor in Lucerne, Ludwig Seiler. When the Lucerne authorities decided to send Seiler to the rural cantons to try to calm things down, the two envoys from Milan travelled with him and visited Brother Klaus. Imperiali spent an evening and a morning with the hermit and in a letter dated 27th June he reported at length to his ducal employer. His introductory remarks include the laconic sentence: 'Brother Klaus is regarded as a saint because he eats nothing.' He goes on:–

> The Confederates have great confidence in him. I found him informed about the whole thing and he said this expression 'named and unnamed' was discreditable. He said he had not yet spoken with the deputies from Unterwalden since their return. I informed him of the honourable and just conditions that your Excellency had offered the Confederates and the trouble Lucerne was taking to obtain their acceptance . . . The affair grieved him sorely and he prayed God would make peace. As I knew that his son was Landamman of Unterwalden I asked the hermit to explain the situation to him. I also wanted the Council to meet, and to have their decision on the question. He said he would send a message in writing to be read at the next Council Meeting, and I had all the afore-mentioned matters explained to him by Gabriel. They (the Councillors of Obwalden) answered that they were in agreement, and would send their representative to the next meeting of the Diet with the instruction that as long as the receipt was worded in a manner consistent with their honour the [claimants] should be paid. We shall see the result on Monday.
>
> The hermit asked me to give his greetings and regards to your Excellency . . . and assured me of his sincere love for you and begged you to overlook minor matters in order to live in peace with the Confederates.
>
> I gave him a length of green satin which he was very pleased with, as he could use it to set off some holy relics formerly belonging to the Duke of Burgundy which the Confederates had recently given him.

In his reply to Imperiali the Duke sent friendly messages to Brother Klaus and expressed his satisfaction that he had been given a suitable present. 'Tell him we will not fail to live in peace with the Confederates as long as it does not touch our honour or that of the state.'

There was no doubt, says Durrer, in his commentary, that the Duke no more wanted war than the Confederates did.

At the Diet in July the offending words were replaced by another formula and after a few further difficulties had been sorted out the affair was regarded as settled although the Duke never actually sealed the document over which there had been so much argument. In October 1483 Imperiali was able to return home, his mission accomplished.

The long letter from Imperiali is the fullest known account of an interview with Brother Klaus on political matters. It suggests a man able to act with confidence and authority. The letter is also of interest for its reference (the only one known) to the holy relics which Brother Klaus had recently been given from the Burgundy treasure. Probably by this time all the precious metal and jewels had been removed, so that a length of opulent Milanese satin to set off the relics would have been doubly pleasing to the old man who was so austere in his own personal life.

While the dispute with Milan was taking its slow course, the climax of the eventful year 1482 at the hermitage in The Ranft was the appointment in October of a permanent chaplain for the chapel. Since 1477 there had been a temporary or visiting chaplain, at one time probably the priest from Horw, neighbouring parish to Heini am Grund in Kriens. But now the gifts that poured in from so many sources – Archduke Sigmund, the authorities in Lucerne and Solothurn and donations from the collecting boxes in the chapel – made it possible to set up a permanent endowment, the terms of which were laid down by Brother Klaus himself. When possible the incumbent was to be a member of Brother Klaus's own family but only if a worthy and suitably qualified candidate were available. He was authorised to assist the parish priest of Sachseln as long as the latter did not exploit him in order to avoid performing his duties conscientiously.

This appointment meant the frequent and regular celebration of mass, which Brother Klaus was able to follow from the small window looking down into the chapel from his cell.

In December the authorities in Berne sent Brother Klaus a gift of 40 pounds for the chapel. After thanking the donors for their generous gift – 'if it had been smaller by half I should still have been pleased', and commending the man who brought the money for his efficient service, he continues:

In love I will write something more. Obedience is the greatest glory that there is in heaven and on earth and therefore you must strive to be obedient to each other; and wisdom is the most valuable for it is the starting point of all things. Peace is in God always, for God is peace and peace should not be disturbed. Where there is unrest peace will be disturbed. See to it therefore that peace is what you stand on, protect widows and orphans as you have done till now.

Avoid public wrong-doing and always stand by righteousness. You must also keep in your hearts God's Passion, for it is man's greatest comfort in his last moments. Many people are in a state of doubt about their faith and the devil makes many attacks on faith – above all in this matter of faith. We must

Oldest painting (1492)

not be in any doubt, for the faith is as it has been revealed. And I do not write this to you because I think you do not believe as you should. I do not doubt that you are good Christians. I write as a warning so that if the evil spirit should attack you you may resist with knightly valour.

That is all. God be with you. Given on St. Martin's Day [4th December] in the year 82. At the end of this letter I have affixed my own seal.

I Brother Klaus

This letter, preserved in the historical museum at Solothurn, has been called Brother Klaus's 'political testament' for it is the nearest thing we have to a general statement on political matters in his own words.

The emphasis on obedience may seem surprising coming from the heartland of Switzerland, where independence had been fought for so stubbornly and was prized so highly, and it is out of tune with 20th century trends, but Brother Klaus had seen what excesses of lawlessness could lead to in his turbulent homeland. In his personal life, obedience meant above all obedience to the guidance of God: everything else stemmed from that. In writing to the Government in Berne he links the need for obedience with the need for wise dealing and righteousness in public affairs. The rather obscure sentence about peace being disturbed where there is unrest (in the original German literally 'unpeace') is probably a compressed way of saying that where there is discontent because of injustice there will be no peace – for true peace is 'always in God'. In those wild and cruel times it was not superfluous to remind the authorities of their duty to protect the weak – widows and orphans in particular. Peace was a by-product of obedience to God and of a caring attitude to God's children.

A constantly recurring political, social and economic problem during Brother Klaus's lifetime and after, was the employment of Swiss soldiers by foreign powers. The most insidious form was the so-called 'pension' system, whereby regular payments were made to leading persons in the cantons in return for providing troops to fight in foreign armies. At its worst this led to the risk of men from the Confederation actually facing each other on the battle field. In addition to the official levies, individuals enlisted independently as mercenaries (this is the origin of the term 'free-lance'). The pressures are understandable – over-population, especially in the infertile mountain regions where the hard conditions developed a tough combative breed; economic need; and the desire for adventure. During the 15th century the Swiss had gained a reputation as the most efficient warriors in Europe, even when outnumbered and defeated, and their services were much sought after. But apart from political complications, the social cost was great. When they returned from foreign service, the soldiers had lost the habit of regular work and were lawless and predatory. The problem occupied the Diet intermittently for decades. Three hundred years later, it was a contingent of Swiss Guards that defended Louis XVI when the Tuileries was stormed. Their gallantry is commemorated by the impressive lion monument in Lucerne, a tourist attraction to this day. A Swiss Guard is still stationed in the Vatican. The fame of these small detachments of personal guards has kept alive the memory of the Swiss as mercenaries, but they are not on a footing, of course, with the troops hired out in the 15th century. There is some scanty evidence that Brother Klaus himself as a young man took part in one such foreign adventure, but in later years he consistently opposed the system. His advice, though often quoted in contemporary chronicles, was disregarded. After his death, his two sons, Hans and Walter, are both recorded as accepting payments for supplying troops, when holding the office of Landammman. The system was not finally abolished until 1859 (an exception being made for the Papal Guard).

The first explicit reference to Brother Klaus's advice to adopt neutrality as a general principle of foreign policy appears in an account of his life by a German historian (Trithemius) writing a quarter of a century after the hermit's death. The most widely quoted version comes from the first printed biography (Salat, 1536) and runs as follows:

> O dear friends, don't make your fence too wide, the better to remain in peace, calm and unity in your honourable and hard-won liberty. Don't burden yourselves with foreign affairs, don't join up with foreign rulers, guard against dissension and self-seeking. Protect your fatherland and cleave to it. Do not foster intentional love of fighting, but if anyone attacks you, then fight bravely for freedom and fatherland.

This homely and practical advice has become an important part of the Brother Klaus tradition. After the decisive defeat of the Confederates at the Battle of Marignano in northern Italy (1515) they ceased to be a formidable element in the power politics of central Europe. From then on Brother Klaus's warning voice was remembered and echoed down the centuries. The relationship between neutrality in foreign policy and as a principle underlying the Covenant of Stans will be considered in more detail in Part Four.

CHAPTER VI

Last Years

IN THE SPRING OF 1482 BROTHER KLAUS was 65 and his total fast had lasted for more than 14 years. His growing reputation laid growing burdens on him. His visitors included an extraordinary assortment of people. To the simple folk asking his advice and the diplomats who openly or by proxy tried to enlist his support must now be added an unforeseen hazard. The situation is described in a letter from the authorities in Obwalden to their opposite numbers in Lucerne. In those days the usual starting point for the journey to The Ranft, at least for foreigners and strangers, was Lucerne, so the authorities there were in a better position to control the movements of would-be visitors than the Landamman in Sarnen, especially as most travellers needed a guide. The place was more remote than can easily be imagined today. It was approached by boat from Lucerne to Stansstad and then, in the words of Hans von Waldheim, over a 'frightful mountain' to Kerns. The direct route did not pass through Sarnen at all.

The Landamman wrote to Lucerne that according to reliable information from Brother Klaus himself and from others:

> a foreign priest had recently visited him and had plagued and troubled him with a very severe examination about the Holy Trinity, the Christian faith and other questions of Christian order. In this trial and ordeal Brother Klaus had shown himself, as we had expected, entirely steadfast, correct and faultless. But the foreign priest, when he could not confound him, uttered threats, and announced he would put someone else on to him who would have to test and examine him even more rigorously.

This was not the first time that such things had been reported to him, the Landamman said, and it angered and troubled the Obwalden authorities no less than Brother Klaus. They asked Lucerne as a matter of urgency to make sure that in future no foreign or unknown persons could visit Brother Klaus unless accompanied by a trustworthy companion who could be relied on to see that the hermit was spared controversial attacks. The expenses of the guide were to be paid, of course, by the intending visitor.

> If we do not do something of this kind and just leave things as they are we are sure that one day some foreign mischief-maker will do Brother Klaus real harm and through this cause us a lot of trouble.

This letter raises some interesting questions. Who were the people who had complained to the Landamman about the disputatious priests? Perhaps his wife, or one of his sons, or his friends who were priests themselves – Oswald Isner or Heini am Grund? Were the authorities in Sarnen also anxious – as the wording seems to suggest – about possibly serious consequences for themselves if Brother Klaus were accused of heresy? The Church might well challenge the right of an untutored layman, however holy, to speak on these controversial matters. One wonders if Brother Klaus was aware of the dangers hanging over his head. Possibly not, but others may have seen more clearly, particularly for instance a well-educated and more travelled man like Heini am Grund. The presence of a third party in any future encounters would be doubly useful – firstly as a witness, and secondly he could if necessary end the interview by suggesting that the old man was getting tired and that the visit had lasted long enough.

A few years later this matter of the disputatious priests had a curious sequel. A certain abbot from a monastery in Germany, accompanied by a fellow abbot, visited Brother Klaus and raised the old familiar controversies.

> The hermit replied to everything precisely and modestly, without the slightest sign of impatience, although he was being hard pressed by the abbot, who was determined to 'get to the bottom' of Brother Klaus and his beliefs. Among other questions he asked: 'Are you the one who boasts not to have eaten for so many years?' The hermit replied: 'Good Father, I have never said and do not say, that I eat nothing.' The abbot persisted and, in the hope of provoking the mild-mannered old man, led the conversation round to covetousness and asked him: 'What is avarice?'

Then Brother Klaus struck:

> 'Why do you ask me, an uneducated man who owns nothing, about avarice, when you learned and rich as you are, not only know better than I do, but have had personal experience of what goes on in an avaricious man's heart? The year before last, in a craze for speculation, you bought 27 measures of best wine for a derisory price and then last year resold it for a huge profit. But your Bishop confounded your cupidity and through his own greed punished yours; in spite of your protests he seized the whole lot by force . . . and removed it to his own cellar and he didn't pay a penny for it and never will. The marks of greed are written on your face and are rooted in your heart and to your mortification have now become obvious.'

> At these words the abbot was dumbfounded and confused and did not reply.

This story is recorded by the German historian Trithemius, who said he got it direct from the other abbot. He confirms that Brother Klaus's accusation was factually correct, but cannot imagine how the hermit in his remote valley could possibly have known of the transaction unless by direct revelation through the Holy Spirit. Writing not long after the event Trithemius did not give the abbot's name, but historical research later identified him. The tale has been delightedly related for 500 years.

Two other anecdotes have frequently been told as further examples of Brother Klaus's clairvoyance. They are of interest even if, as in the case of the avaricious abbot, it is not impossible to imagine an alternative source of information to the Holy Spirit. What they do illuminate – in contrast to his formidable qualities when roused to wrath – is his kindly manner towards the young and the unhappy.

When young Nicholas, Brother Klaus's youngest son, was studying in Paris, he entrusted two letters to a fellow-student to take to his father in Switzerland. During the long journey home, the student lost one of the letters and was so afraid Brother Klaus would be angry that he hardly dared to deliver the second letter. However, he plucked up courage and made his way to The Ranft. Before he reached the hermitage, Brother Klaus came down the slope to meet him, holding a letter in his hand. He greeted him kindly and showed him the letter – it was the one he had lost. The young man was unable to imagine how Brother Klaus could have received the letter or recognised him from afar, but his main reaction was relief and gratitude for the warmth of his welcome. He himself told the story to Brother Klaus's biographer, Wölflin. Presumably Brother Klaus knew from the letter he already had that Nicholas's friend would be arriving with another one.

The other story concerns a married woman in the neighbouring village of Kerns who was convinced that her husband was being unfaithful. She had thoughts of killing the other woman and in great distress of mind she decided to seek help from Brother Klaus, but when she arrived at The Ranft there were such crowds both in the chapel and going in and out of his cell that it was impossible to have a word with him alone. Just as she was thinking of giving up and going home, Brother Klaus strode into the chapel and said, addressing no one in particular, 'There is a woman here who wants my advice. She can go home in peace. Her suspicions are unjust. The couple are innocent.' Having said this, he returned to his cell.

This anecdote is not found in the earliest records but if the tradition is accepted as substantially accurate, it incidentally throws light on the pressures on Brother Klaus, and gives an ironical twist to the frequent references by all the early chroniclers to his choosing to live in the 'Einöde' (wilderness or solitary place). The appointment of a resident chaplain must have increased even further the number of people visiting the chapel, now that mass could be regularly held and was not dependent on the occasional services of a visiting or temporary priest. There is a tradition that Brother Klaus used to appear at his little window overlooking the chapel after mass and greet the congregation with a blessing: 'The name of Jesus be your greeting! I wish you a happy day!'

In the last years of his life the spotlight moves to his family and friends. In 1483 his son Hans, now in his mid-thirties, was elected to the high position of Landamman in Obwalden. In 1486-7 he was suspected of involvement in a plot against the foreign city of Lindau. A rich merchant had managed at some stage in his colourful career to acquire Landrecht (that is, rights of nationality) in Unterwalden and when he got into trouble outside their territory he claimed protection. A gang of hot-headed men from Unterwalden, in defiance of the Stans agreement, took the law into their own hands and by their ill-judged behaviour threatened the peace of the whole Confederation. At a late stage in the long-drawn-out affair Hans von Flüe was accused of complicity in acts of arson in Lindau and two other cities beyond the Swiss border. Brother Klaus was obviously not involved in the beligerent activities of his fellow countrymen, although possibly a visit to him in 1482 by an official from the authorities in Lucerne may have been to seek his moderating influence. His name crops up in the affair, however, for in the publicity surrounding it Hans von Flüe is frequently described as 'Brother Klaus's son'. It must have grieved the old man that his son was accused of unlawful activities – whether justly or not is unknown. The evidence implicating him was obtained under torture.

Robert Durrer in his notes on the career of Hans von Flüe suggests that the gradual disappearance of any mention of Brother Klaus's name in connection with political matters towards the end of his life may be not unconnected with his sons' growing influence. Neither Hans nor Walter were in sympathy with their father's position on the question of foreign levies (the 'pensions') and probably not with his far-seeing and unparochial attitude to constitutional matters. But the hermit was growing old, and as his hopes turned towards release from earthly cares, perhaps he himself, or those nearest him, began to discourage burdensome visitors.

Meanwhile, in the year that Hans was first elected Landamman, Klaus's youngest son, Nicholas, now 16, became a student at Basel University. About this time also a chapel was built in Mösli for Klaus's neighbour, Brother Ulrich. Towards the end of 1484 there was yet another outbreak of trouble with the incumbent of Sachseln. Brother Klaus can hardly have avoided hearing all about it, but there is no record of any personal involvement.

As we have seen, the hermit received many unsolicited gifts, and this enabled him, though possessing so little, to subscribe to various good causes, which no doubt gave him pleasure. One such gift was to the chapel of St. Joden in Altsellen, near his mother's birthplace. But his association with good causes led to abuses. Sometimes collections were dishonestly made in his name – there are two records of swindlers being punished for this.

Few details are known of his last illness. He suffered acute pain in all his limbs and because of his extreme emaciation could find no way to lie in comfort. His only bed, apart from a narrow plank against the wall with a stone for a pillow, was the floor. It is surmised and one certainly hopes, that his inward guide let him accept the presence of his wife to nurse him. 'Surely God would allow us this last mercy' is his reply, in one fictional account, to her whispered request to remain. Perhaps one of the married daughters also came, Frau Hensli Grisinger (her Christian name is not known) who lived quite near, or Dorothea or Verena from Altsellen, near Engelberg, or his daughter-in-law Elsbeth von Einwil, whose father had lent him a seal when first he needed one for his letters. On the eighth day of his illness he asked for the last sacraments and when he had received them he breathed his last, uttering a thanksgiving. It was his seventieth birthday, 21st March 1487.

The news of his death travelled fast and a huge crowd attended his funeral in Sachseln. All the neighbouring churches were closed so that their parish priests could attend. His earthly remains were laid first in the churchyard; today, encased in gold, they lie in front of the altar in the 17th century church. But of course this is not where Brother Klaus can best be found. In the words of Robert Durrer 'the life of a saint does not end with his death, often its real significance only begins then.'

PART TWO

The Eyewitnesses

NEIGHBOURS, FRIENDS AND FAMILY

These six testimonies are from the 'Churchbook of Sachseln' (Kirchenbuch von Sachseln), which is one of the most important sources of first-hand knowledge about Brother Klaus, especially about his life before he became a hermit. They were recorded about 18 months after his death, perhaps with canonisation in mind, although they are not in the strict legal form required by the Catholic authorities. It is not known who initiated the enquiry and actually wrote them down. It may have been the anonymous author of the Pilgertraktat.

There is no mention of Brother Klaus's peacemaking role at Stans or other involvement in public affairs, probably because his immediate family did not share his views.

From ERNY ROHRER OF UNTERWALDEN

Erny Rohrer of Unterwalden, over 80 years old, or thereabouts, said that from youth he had always associated with Brother Klaus and had been his intimate friend and neighbour for 40 years. They had often been together since they were small boys and later they used to go to the fields or otherwise work together and Brother Klaus had always been a retiring, virtuous, good, pious and sincere man who never caused offence to anyone. And when they came home from the fields or other work, Brother Klaus would go off by himself behind a cowshed or to some other lonely place. There he would pray, leaving him [Erny] and the other boys to run off where they liked. He also always directed them and his brothers and sisters and the neighbours to good works and himself practised many austerities. He began this when he was still quite a young boy and for a long time fasted every Friday, later four days a week, as well as the whole [Lenten] fast when he would eat nothing all day but a small piece of bread or a few dried pears. But he did this secretly, so as not to show off. And if he was asked about it, or reproached by some who thought he would not be able to bear it, he always said: God will have it so. *(Gott will es so haben.)* Where possible he withdrew from the world, fled from and scorned all worldly honours and in particular he made strenuous efforts to avoid becoming Landamman which he would otherwise have become in due course.

He also said that Brother Klaus had often told him how the Devil plagued him daily, but our Dear Lady always comforted him, as also when at one time he intended to go abroad, leaving wife, child and farm and end his days in a foreign land.

When at that time he came towards Liestal it seemed to him that the whole town and everything in it was all red, at which he drew back in fear. He turned off the path and made his way to a farmhouse and talked to the farmer, to whom after some conversation he told what he had in mind, which the good farmer did not approve of, but on the contrary advised him against it, and thought he ought to return to his own people and serve God there. That would be more pleasing to God than becoming a burden to strangers; he would also have a more peaceful time, on the grounds that he was a Confederate to whom not all of them were friendly. Therefore that same night he left the farmhouse for the fields. He lay there overnight under a hedge and when he fell asleep there came a glow and a beam of light from the heavens which pierced his belly causing a pain like being cut open with a knife. This showed him that he was to go back to The Ranft and in the morning he at once did so. When he reached home he remained for eight days up in the Melchaa valley, among the brambles and wild undergrowth, but when he was discovered, people came pestering him and gave him no peace. Then, as he later told him [Erny Rohrer] and others, he saw four bright lights in the sky which showed him the place where they should build him a dwelling and a chapel which was done at his desire according to his revelation. [This is a rather telescoped account of a process that took some time.] There Brother Klaus had his dwelling until his death, served God and as he [Erny Rohrer] firmly believed lived without any food or drink for twenty and a half years, loved righteousness, advanced the truth and rebuked evil.

Even in war he did his enemies little injury but stood aside, prayed and protected them as far as possible.

From ERNY ANDERHALDEN OF UNTERWALDEN

Erny Anderhalden of Unterwalden, above the Forest, 75 years old or thereabouts, said that from childhood days till now he had always associated with Brother Klaus. He [Klaus] had always loved fair dealing and rebuked injustice and in war did little injury to his enemies, but spared them as far as possible. He was always God-fearing and very devout and prayed frequently and devoutly, practised many austerities and for a long time fasted every Friday, later four days a week, and the whole (Lenten) fast as well, ate nothing but a small piece of bread or a few dried pears once a day. He also fled from and despised all worldly power and honours, seeking nothing but God's honour, and in particular exerted himself so that at his earnest plea the parish council released him from his positions as magistrate and councillor.

Further Brother Klaus once told him that when he was 16 years old he had seen a beautiful high tower in the place where his hermitage and chapel now stand. For this reason from youth up he had always been willing to seek solitude.

The Devil had troubled him greatly especially once, when he was about to cut back brambles in the high meadow in Melchtal, the Devil had hurled him with such force over a boundary ridge into a big thicket that he lost consciousness and was otherwise injured, he Erny Anderhalden, having seen the marks on his body. And Brother Klaus had also told him more than once that God had granted him, among others, three great mercies, namely, first that he obtained the agreement of his wife and children to his life as a hermit, secondly that he never had any wish, longing or temptation to return to his wife and children from this life and thirdly that he was able to live without bodily food and drink, as he [Erny Anderhalden] firmly believed, (namely) Brother Klaus took no bodily food or drink for twenty and a half years, for he had never seen, or heard of or perceived such a thing. Furthermore Brother Klaus had never spoken or done any evil, for he had always lived according to God's will, always devoted himself to all good things and also advised his children, neighbours, friends and others in the same way.

From HEINI AM GRUND (1431 or earlier to 1493)

Parish Priest Kriens (near Lucerne) 1465-81, Stans 1481-93.

He belonged to a respected family established in Lucerne, but possibly originating from Engelberg or elsewhere in Unterwalden. After his death his brother Gilg had a dispute with the Monastery of Engelberg over the possession of his library. Heini was probably a member of the movement known as the 'Friends of God'. Some years younger than Brother Klaus he was his close friend and adviser and played an important role at several critical moments in his life.

Herr Heini am Grund, parish priest of Stans, said that Brother Klaus had told him that in his mother's womb, before he was born, he had seen a star in the heavens which lit up the whole world, and since he had lived in The Ranft he had constantly seen a star like it in the sky, so that he firmly believed that this star was himself. That meant, as he explained, that everyone would be able to say of him that he shone thus in the world.

Brother Klaus also told him that before his birth, in his mother's womb, he had seen a great stone, which meant the steadfastness and constancy with which he should persevere and not give up his undertaking. And at the same time when in his mother's womb he had seen the Holy Oil and when he was born and came into the world he had recognised his mother and the midwife and saw himself being carried through The Ranft to Kerns with such clarity that he had never forgotten it, for he still saw it today as well as when it actually happened. At the same time he saw an old man standing by the font whom he didn't know, but the priest who baptised him, Klaus knew quite well.

He also told him that when he intended to go abroad and was approaching Liestal the town and everything in it seemed to him all red, which caused him to hurry away and go to a solitary farmhouse, to a farmer to whom, among other things, he told his plans but the farmer was against it, and advised him to go back to his own people and serve God there; that would be better than staying with strangers, for he would have more peace at home, because he was a Confederate to whom not everybody was friendly, whereupon he left the farmer's house that same evening and lay down overnight by a hedge in the fields. And after he fell asleep there came a glow and a beam of light from the sky; this cut his belly open which caused him as much pain as if he had been cut by a knife and showed him that he should go back home to The Ranft and serve God there, which is what he did.

From the PARISH PRIEST OF KERNS

Father Oswald Isner's testimony is one of the most important contemporary records, especially in connection with the fast. Except for the first paragraph (below) it has already been quoted in full on page 10 (consultation at the beginning of the fast) and page 18 (Klaus derives strength from witnessing the sacrament of the Eucharist).

The passages are repeated here in one uninterrupted narrative in order to present the six eyewitness accounts from the Churchbook as a single unabridged whole.

Item, Herr Oswald Isner, Parish Priest of Kerns, said that he had always been intimate with Brother Klaus and had frequently visited him in his hermitage and that he [Klaus] had often complained to him that he had suffered many attacks from the Evil Spirit and in particular once the Devil came to him (as it seemed to him) in the form of a nobleman, in richly ornamented clothes, and after a long talk advised him to give up his undertaking and act like other people, for he would not gain eternal life by his present ways. Also Brother Klaus had often told him why he had left home to go abroad and how near Liestal he had been turned back by a farmer and by a fiery glow and told to go home to The Ranft. That was the time he had begun to abstain from natural food and he had persisted for 11 days.

Then Brother Klaus had sent for him and asked his advice in confidence whether he should eat or whether to go on with the experiment, for he had always longed to live without food and thus be more independent of the world. Whereupon he had felt Brother Klaus's leg above and below on which there was very little flesh, for he was wasted away to the skin, his cheeks quite thin and his lips quite shrunken. And when he had satisfied himself that Klaus's fast was truly based on and justified by his love for God, he advised him that since God had allowed him to hold out without food for 11 days, then as long as he could stand it without starving to death, he could try for still longer, which is what Brother Klaus did, and from then on for twenty and a half years to the end of his life persisted in taking no bodily food whether by eating or drinking. And as Brother Klaus had perhaps been closer to him than to anyone else and he had greatly wondered what kept him alive, he had often asked Brother Klaus and pressed him about it for a long time and once in his little house he had told him in great confidence that when he was present at mass, and the priest partook of the sacrament, he [Klaus] obtained a strength from this that enabled him to live without food or drink – otherwise he could not have borne it.

From HANS VON FLÜE

Hans von Flüe, Brother Klaus's legitimate son, Landamman of Unterwalden, above the Forest, over 40 years old, said that as long as he could remember his father had always shunned the world and had a hermitlike disposition and at all times, striving for peace, had punished wrongdoing with great disapproval and loved righteousness; also he fasted every week four days, namely, Monday, Wednesday, Friday and Saturday and throughout all fast days he ate no more than one small piece of bread or a few dried pears all day long, otherwise took nothing warm nor anything else. In the evening he always went to bed at the same time as his family but every night if ever he [Hans] woke he would hear that his father had got up again and was praying in the living room by the stove, until [the time when] he went to The Ranft. He also always despised all worldly power and honour and never desired anything but to serve God in solitude; the Devil had often caused him much pain and unrest. Once especially when he went with his father to the high meadow in Melchtal, while he was seeing to the cattle his father wanted to hack away the brambles and clean up the meadow; at that moment the Devil came and hurled his father a good 30 paces through a great bramble thicket and down a boundary-ridge so that he lost consciousness and did not know where he was; when he [Hans] got

41

there he lifted his father up and carried him senseless to the fire [in their living quarters in the cow-stall], and when after some time he came to himself he was quite uncomplaining, although he was in very poor shape, and all he said was, 'Oh well, in God's name, the Devil certainly did me a bad turn, but I suppose it must have been God's will.'

From WALTER VON FLÜE

Walter von Flüe, standard-bearer, of Unterwalden, said that Brother Klaus had once told him that one time at the beginning of his break [with the world] he was going to mow in Melchi [a meadow below Flüeli, not the high meadow in the Melchtal to which Hans refers] and on the way he prayed to God to grant him a holy life. Then there came a cloud from heaven which spoke to him and said he should submit to God's will, he was a foolish man and he should be willing to do what God wanted him to do and that he had done right to surrender to God's will.

These two testimonies from Klaus's sons are given in full. In the light of all that is known of Brother Klaus's life they are as remarkable for what they do not say as for what they regard as worthy of mention. The circumstances in which they made their statements are not known. If they were aware what the other witnesses had said they may have deliberately avoided repetition. But Hans's mention of his father punishing evil-doing with great displeasure arouses some speculation.

AN INTERRUPTED NARRATIVE: THE DOMINICAN FRIAR

This fragment was found in an appendix to an old quarto in the City Archives in Lucerne.

A certain brother from a preaching order [visited] the pious and devout Brother Nikolaus of Flü (sic) in Unterwalden on Corpus Christi day and the Friday following [8th and 9th June] in the year 1469 and after several talks on spiritual matters, he exhorted him to guard against the spirit of arrogance, and supported this with many reasons from the Scriptures and the sayings of the saints. He replied that he never or seldom felt troubled by this. So then the friar asked the above-named brother [Klaus] by what steps and deserving deeds he had achieved what was said of him, namely that he lived without earthly food – and if it was true? He replied: 'This is a difficult question, for I have revealed it to no one except a pious priest from Lucerne, but if you will promise not to let it be known before my death, I will trust to your conscience.' When the above-mentioned brother heard this, he said: 'Perhaps I shall die before you.' Brother Klaus replied: 'I don't think you will die before me.' Then the brother promised not to reveal the secret before Brother Klaus's death. Whereupon Brother Klaus began his story and said: 'When I was a young man, I took a wife and was powerful as a magistrate and councillor and in the affairs of my fatherland here. And I cannot remember ever having departed from the path of justice in my dealings with anyone; of all humankind I most valued and honoured the royal and priestly folk – that is to say Christ's priests, so that whenever I saw a priest it was as if I saw one of God's angels. It was first through this, I think, that I came to hold in such reverence and honour the blessed sacrament of the body and blood of Jesus Christ.

'When then it pleased him for the sake of my redemption to extend his full mercy towards me he made use of the purifying file and the goad to drive me on – that is, a deep affliction and trial, so that I had no peace by day or by night, but was brought so low that even my dear wife and the company of my children were a burden to me. While I remained in this state the confidant and close friend whom I previously mentioned – and to whom I revealed that secret – came to see me and we had an important talk. We spoke of all sorts of things and I revealed my anxiety and trouble to him. He offered various remedies and suggestions by which he hoped to lift my affliction but I replied: "I've tried those and similar things and found no comfort – they haven't helped me in the least." But finally he produced the best and most powerful remedy: there remained (he said) the devout contemplation of the passion of Christ. Quite encouraged, I replied that I knew nothing of a special method or way of contemplating Christ's passion. Then he taught me how to divide the contemplation of the passion into parts according to the seven canonical hours and the daily liturgy of the Church. Whereupon I began this way of contemplation and carried out these exercises every day, in which I made progress through the compassion of the Saviour for my pitiful state; but because I was involved in many worldly affairs and official responsibilities I found that in the company of other people my concentration was not complete. Therefore I withdrew to this nearby secret place and no one knew of it but my wife and then only by accident. And so I remained for two years . . .'

Here the Mss breaks off suddenly.

ARISTOCRAT FROM NORTH GERMANY: HANS VON WALDHEIM (1422-79)

Hans von Waldheim of Halle had held various high positions in local government. Well-educated, happily married, one son. In 1474-5 he spent a year on a pilgrimage to shrines in the south of France. Political disturbances in Halle as well as piety and intellectual curiosity may have prompted the journey. His visit to Brother Klaus was in May 1474 when he was crossing Switzerland on his way home. On his return he found his patrican party overthrown and his personal liberty in danger and he spent the last four years of his life in Leipzig.

He had an observant eye and recorded his impressions while they were fresh in his mind. There are a few minor inaccuracies, – for instance, Brother Klaus did not go direct to The Ranft, the Bishop of Constance did not come in person, – but they are small points such as might easily arise through misunderstandings in the course of a long conversation. Durrer says that Dorothy was almost certainly more than 40. In the main von Waldheim is a careful and accurate reporter whose account tallies substantially with verifiable facts and with the biography by Wölflin, who did not know of the Journal and based his work on local tradition. Waldheim's Journal only became available to Brother Klaus researchers in 1826.

I left my horses at Lucerne, hired a boat and on Wednesday, Pope Urban's Day [25th May] I travelled up the Lake of Lucerne to Brother Klaus, the living saint.

When we had travelled a good two miles up the lake, we came to a frightful mountain. We couldn't believe people really lived there. We had to climb up this mountain, difficult and hazardous as it was. There was neither path nor track and the forest torrents came rushing towards us. But when we got to the top we found a really lovely countryside, with villages, good arable land, meadows, forests and also good pastures. Also fine cattle, cows, oxen and horses, particularly handsome stallions. This is also the country of the finest hawks in the world. Even the Duke of Milan has hawks brought him from here every year. This high-lying land is called Unterwalden, and is inhabited by good, German-speaking folk.

43

After this we came to a village called Kerns. The inn belonged to the Amman (magistrate), unter der Flüe. As I was sitting in the inn parlour, the innkeeper sat down beside me and said: 'Good Sir, what has brought you to our country? Have you come to see Brother Klaus?' So I said: 'Yes'. The innkeeper answered: 'It is not easy to get to see him, for he doesn't see just anybody who comes. But if you really want to meet him, I'll give you my advice and tell you what I think, otherwise it will hardly be possible to get to see him. We have in this village a parish priest, our pastor, who is Brother Klaus's confessor; if you could persuade him to go with you, he could take you to him, to see him and talk to him.' I at once asked the innkeeper to send someone to the priest and invite him to be my guest at supper. This was done. While we were sitting over the meal, I told him that I had ridden from a far-off country and a great distance. In my country I had heard of a living saint called Brother Klaus, who had eaten and drunk nothing for six years. That was why I had come to see him. I had been told that he was his confessor and that it would only be possible to meet Brother Klaus with his help. I sincerely hoped he would not be put out if I asked him to travel to Brother Klaus with me tomorrow, Thursday. He replied he would be glad to do so. Then the innkeeper spoke: 'Good sir, you mustn't go on foot. I'll lend you a grey horse to ride – I have three fine horses in my stable and you can take your pick.'

On the Thursday after Exaudi (the Sunday after Ascension Day), the parish priest was ready early with me, my servant and my boatmen. We travelled half a mile – in our country it would have been a good mile. When we had covered about half the distance to Brother Klaus the priest asked me if I would like to see Brother Klaus's wife as well. I said yes. He showed me a house on an airy hilltop across a deep valley and said that was where Brother Klaus used to live and where his wife and youngest son still lived; the older sons, who were already married, lived not far off. He said to the boat boy: 'Run over to Brother Klaus's wife and tell her I'll be holding mass and if they want to hear it she should come and bring the youngest boy along with her.'

We went on and reached Brother Klaus's cell. The Swiss have built a chapel onto it with three altars. As we were standing in the chapel the priest asked me which mass I would like to have read. I replied: 'St. Mary Magdalena.' The priest went to the altar and looked up the office for St. Mary Magdalena and when he had found it he turned round and saw Brother Klaus's wife and her son. I gave her and the boy my hand and wished them good morning. His wife is still a good-looking young woman of under 40, fresh-faced with a smooth skin. I asked her 'Dear lady, how long has Brother Klaus been gone?' She replied, 'This boy here, my son, will be seven years old on St. John the Baptist Day [24th June] and when he was 13 weeks old – it was on St. Gallus Day – Brother Klaus parted from me and he has never been with me since.' I had quite a lot more talk with her and the son. The boy has an upright carriage like Brother Klaus and he is the image of his father. I gave him a small present of money (Lit. 'Trinkgeld' – a tip).

One should bear in mind that Brother Klaus left his wife in the year of our Lord 1467, St. Gallus Day. He parted from her with the firm intention of going abroad and of wandering as a 'Forest Brother' from one holy place to another. With this intention he took leave of his wife and set off on foot; but when he was approaching Basel, he received a vision, a revelation and a warning from God so that he turned back from Basel and returned to Unterwalden and his home. However, he didn't speak to his wife, nor his children, nor anyone else, but stayed overnight in a

44

cowshed near his farmhouse. In the morning he got up early and went some way further into the nearby forest. He made himself a small shelter of wood and foliage. When the Swiss realised that Brother Klaus intended to spend his life in that place they felled big trees in the forest and built a chapel with three altars and a little house against it where he now lives and leads a holy life.

From the day when he parted from his wife Brother Klaus has neither eaten nor drunk.

Brother Klaus is a well-built man of my age, in the prime of life, approaching 50 years old. His hair is brown, still no grey. He has well-formed, good-looking features, a rather narrow face and is of slim, upright build. He has a pleasant voice and speaks German well.

He used to be a respected holder of public office. He also took part in several major battles.

There follows a brief report on the check on his fast as related elsewhere.

Brother Klaus has his hermitage in Unterwalden in a remote place at the foot of the Alps, on which chamois and ibex, very valuable and high-class game, live and leap.

Brother Klaus is in the habit of frequently going off into the wild forest for a day or two when he wants to be alone for his time of contemplation.

The people here also say that he is often seen at the shrine of our dear lady at Einsiedeln, but no one meets him on the way, either going or returning. How or by what paths he goes is known to almighty God, no doubt.

Before I visited Brother Klaus, I was told that he had no natural bodily warmth, but that his hands felt ice-cold and that his face was yellower and paler than a corpse ready for the grave. Also that he was always in a sad humour and never cheerful. But I must say that I didn't find any of these characteristics. In the first place his hands were warm, like other people's. Both of us, my servant Kunze and I, touched his hands four or five times as later recorded. His face was not yellow and pale, but had a natural flesh tint just like other living people in good health. Nor was he of a sad disposition, but in his conversation, behaviour and way of doing things we found him affable, communicative, at ease and, above all, friendly.

. . . I first heard of Brother Klaus in the following way: Henry von Waldheim, my son, asked me on Mary's birthday [8th October] in the year of our Lord 1473 if I could buy some good strings for his lute at the Annual Fair in Halle in Saxony. So I went to the Fair with him and we came to a merchant selling all sorts of wares, including many precious stones, and I bought the strings for him. We talked for a long time about precious stones. Then he asked me if I had ever heard of the living saint, Brother Klaus by name. He had his hermitage in Unterwalden in Switzerland and for many years he had neither eaten nor drunk. When I got home I wrote this in my journal in the hope and intention, if I ever came to that country to ask about him.

The second time I heard of Brother Klaus happened in the following way: on Ascension Day Thursday in the year of our Lord 1474 I came to Berne and stayed at the Bell Inn. Here I met the prior of the Carthusian Monastery of Eisenach. He had visited Brother Klaus and told me a lot about him.

To return to our description and the object of it: the parish priest of Kerns celebrated the Mass of St. Mary Magdalena for God and for us. When the Mass was over, the priest, Brother Klaus's confessor, took me and my servant to Brother Klaus's hermitage, which adjoins the chapel. When we came to him in his little room Brother Klaus, with a friendly smile, offered us his hand, which was not cold, but of natural warmth. After this, he requested our patience for a moment as he wanted to say a few words to the people who had been attending the service. He went towards the chapel, opened the glass window and said 'God grant you a good and blessed morning, dear friends and dear people.' He closed the window again and sat down beside us. I told him how I had come from a distant land to the shrines of Saint Mary Magdalena, Saint Anna and Saint Antonius, and the other beloved saints . . . and now I had also come to him. When he heard this, he said: 'I had my chapel consecrated in honour of Saint Mary Magdalena.' So I told him the whole story of Saint Mary Magdalena coming across the sea to Marseilles and how she lived in a cave and was lifted in the air seven times a day by the holy angels and also how she departed this life and was buried at Saint Maximin, where the shrine was called after her; I told him all about this until he was moved to tears. After this he gave us much loving, godly teaching. Then I spoke again: 'Dear Brother Klaus, at home in our country, and also here, I have heard that you neither eat nor drink and that you haven't eaten or drunk for many years – is this so?' He replied, 'God knows,' and continued, 'Some people said that the life I was leading was not from God but from the Evil Spirit. Therefore my Lord of Constance, the Bishop, blessed and consecrated three pieces of bread and also some Saint Johannes wine in the belief that if I ate the bread that had been blessed and drank the blessed holy drink that would be a sign that all was well with me, but if I didn't eat the bread and drink the wine, that would be a genuine sign that my affairs and my life were of the devil.

'Among many other things my Lord the Bishop of Constance, asked me what was the best and most deserving virtue in a holy Christian life. I answered and said it was holy obedience. Then my Lord Bishop said: "Well, if obedience is the best and most deserving of all the virtues, I command you in the name of holy obedience to eat these three small pieces of bread and drink this Saint Johannes wine." I begged my Lord, the Bishop, to spare me and let me off, because it would be difficult and painful for me. I asked this more than once. But he would not grant it, and out of obedience I had to eat the bread and drink the wine.' On hearing this I said to Brother Klaus: 'Have you eaten or drunk since that time?' I received no answer but, 'God knows.' After much further talk I took leave of him, asking him to remember me in his prayers. He gave us his hand and we took leave of him.

One more thing: after we had left him, I had forgotten something I wanted to speak to him about. I asked the priest, his confessor, if he could arrange for me to meet him once more. This was done and we three went to him again. He received us with outstretched hand. I said what I wanted to say and again took leave of him, offering my hand.

As we were still standing in the porch of the chapel, Brother Klaus came towards us from his cell and called to the priest, his confessor. They spoke quietly together. I don't know what. Then we left him and went away.

The priest then led them by steep and rocky ways further up the valley to Brother Ulrich.

Brother Ulrich has a cell but no chapel, just a small anteroom in which there were many pictures of the passion of our Lord, and pictures of saints. Near the hermitage a spring gushes out of the rocks. Brother Ulrich is a small man and eats no more in the day than three small pieces of bread dipped in water. He lives with great moderation and drinks nothing.

Brother Ulrich took us into his cell and showed us his belongings and the books he reads, for he is educated, whereas Brother Klaus is a simple layman and cannot read.

I mounted my horse and rode with my companion to my inn, where I had ordered a meal for us. When we arrived at the inn, my host, the Amman, asked me if I had seen Brother Klaus and what I had thought of him. I told him all that had happened and that I regarded Brother Klaus as a truly good man and a living saint, and said that in my opinion he would work many wonders after his death . . . After we had eaten I did my accounts and paid my bill at the inn. I also made a gift to the priest and gave him a donation for charity and thanked him for his trouble and for taking us to see Brother Klaus. I also thanked the innkeeper and his wife for their good hospitality. We climbed down the mountain again, got into our boat and travelled the same route over the lake to Lucerne, where my horses were waiting.

AN OBSERVANT CLERIC: DEAN ALBRECHT VON BONSTETTEN

Albrecht von Bonstetten's account was originally written in Latin and later translated into German. It was addressed to various notabilities and was written for immediate publication, unlike Hans von Waldheim's personal journal. The date of the visit was 31st December 1478.

After recommending the report to the careful attention of his readers, he describes the Canton of Unterwalden and gives a summary of the main events of Brother Klaus's life, his marriage, the birth of 'well-built children of both sexes', the high opinion in which he was held locally, his abstemious life and 'following the gospel', his decision to leave 'his wife, his children, his house and all that he held dear.' He gives an account of the watch set to test the genuineness of his fast and the building of the chapel and the adjoining dwelling where he now lives. He continues:

As these things were talked of everywhere, I also was moved by the wish to see him and in fulfilment of this wish I set off with a worthy company and made haste to visit him in his wilderness. What the place was like, what I saw, what he was like in body, face, words and manners, dear gentlemen and good friends, I will set before you as well as I can. This is how the place is situated: we came through the forest to a village called Kerns, towards Brünig, the previously mentioned mountain; shortly before leaving the village we left the broad track and bore more to the left towards the icy, lofty, snow-covered alps, and after climbing these mountains and hills about half a mile we came to a plateau through which a rapidly running stream flowed out of the mountain-side with great whirling and roaring. From there we went down to the bottom of a steep slope and from there upstream about 500 paces. On our right, only a stone's throw from the stream lay the hermitage at the foot of the gorge.

We went to the chapel which was well provided with the things that are needed for the service, and was also ornamented with pictures and statues . . . We asked the priest whom we had brought with us to perform the office, which we listened to humbly kneeling, and the Brother took part behind us, as was his custom, through a small window. Then the Landamman, who was a relative of Brother Klaus and who had kindly accompanied us here, climbed the staircase and asked permission for us to meet and talk with him, which he soon obtained. So then we also went to him. The cell is on two floors, one above the other. The servant of God awaited us in the upper

47

part and when he saw us he spoke softly and modestly in a manly voice, barefoot, upright: 'Greetings to you, beloved Fathers and Brothers in God,' and gave us his hand in correct fashion.

We thanked him, all quite overcome, and really my hair stood on end and my voice failed me. He went on, 'Why have you come to this remote gorge in this wild place? Just so that you could see me, a poor sinner? I am afraid you will find nothing in me worthy of a visit from such people as you.'

With one accord we said: 'Yes – everything that is pleasing to almighty God, a knight of Jesus Christ and God's servant.' 'Would to God that were so', he replied again; after a few more words he said, 'Come down into the warm.' 'After you, Father,' we said, 'we will follow you.' We asked him about various things and he answered not as if trying to make an impression but in general as befitted an unlearned but exceptional and outstanding man, so that he would have compelled respect even from an enemy. I had a good look round to take everything in and to observe exactly his person and the room. He is tall, very thin, brown and wrinkled, with uncombed hair, black mixed with grey, not very thick. His beard is about a thumb's length. He has medium-sized eyes, with very clear whites, well-preserved teeth and a nose that goes well with his face. He is not talkative, and reserved with strangers. I judge him to be about 60. If you touch him, his skin is cold. He is bare-headed and barefoot and wears nothing on his bare body but a grey robe. The room was slightly warm on St. Silvester's Day [31st December]. It has two very small windows and no adjacent room or any kind of concealed sleeping place except that already mentioned.

I saw no domestic utensils, no table and no bed on which the servant of God could have lain. He has to stand or sit, or lie on the floor of the little room, if he wants to rest.

Finally we enquired about his fellow-hermit, Brother Ulrich, whom he praised highly and urged us also to visit before we left this wild place. We agreed, and now the time had come to take our leave so that we should not outstay our welcome. We thanked him, asked him to remember us in his prayers, and left.

There follows a descripton of the visit to Brother Ulrich.

With this, I have briefly summarised what I saw with my own eyes. I will now tell you briefly what I heard from trustworthy people. They said it was now the fourteenth year that Brother Klaus had eaten nothing, except once in obedience to the Suffragen Bishop of Constance, when the chapel was consecrated, three small pieces of bread and some consecrated St. John's wine. They also said that he sleeps half standing, leaning against a wall. At the beginning of his hermit's life the Evil One had afflicted him grievously so that he was often found lying half dead. Every day, especially in summer, he goes to a cave about three hours away, in order to pray.

He sets great store by obedience and peace and always urged the Confederates and everyone who came to him to keep the peace. Some also say that he has prophesied future events but I neither heard this from him nor anything further about it from others. His life is so full of devotion and virtue that I have complete confidence in him and believe only good of him and do not let myself be confused by what others say. What does it matter? One should just remember that it is rightly written: so many men, so many minds.

You have now, dear gentlemen and dear friends this hermit's life and manners briefly sketched . . .

SEEKING ADVICE: THE YOUNG MAN FROM BURGDORF

The oldest surviving copy of this letter (mid-16th century) is in the City Archives in Lucerne. It is in Latin, but the reference to dancing is in dialect in the original. The date of the young man's visit must have been after the arrival of Brother Ulrich and was probably before the appointment of a permanent chaplain (1482). But the letter was written some years later, after Brother Klaus's death. The signature is missing and nothing is known of the young man's subsequent career. The journey from Burgdorf on foot to The Ranft would have taken an active young man two or three days.

Concerning Brother Klaus of Obwalden, my dearly beloved in the Lord Jesus, who died on St. Benedict's Day, 1487.

The eternal blessing of the Lord be with you! Dear Walter, my brother!

It is your pious wish that I should write an account for you of what Brother Nicholas of Flüe said to me. I will do what you ask, but I was seized with confusion at the sight of him and therefore only dared to ask so little of this great man. However it consoles me to think that this remarkable character has had many conversations with those who are accustomed to ask a lot of questions. I have heard this from other people.

The first time I visited him I asked only one question, namely: Would it be right for me to remain in this place to serve God, although my parents knew nothing of my intention, so that my conscience was not clear? The man of God replied briefly: 'If you intend to serve God, you must pay no heed to anyone. But if you just think it would be nice to spend your days here then you would do better to stay with your own folk, and support them.' Satisfied with this answer, I went away, in my stupidity asking him nothing more, neither about God nor godly things, for I was not yet a son, only a poor slave, and fear closed the door to a more intimate approach; but God has willed that so far I have not been an unfaithful son!

Meanwhile, however, after I had returned to Burgdorf and turned over and over in my mind what state I should choose in order to serve God, I went there [to The Ranft] again. But when I reached his hermitage to ask advice of the man of God I couldn't find him. I waited for a long time before he came and when I hastened towards him he held out his hand and said 'Welcome'. I replied, 'You are welcome to me too, I'd been hoping you'd arrive for so long', and I added, 'I visited you some time ago and asked if I might stay here in this place to serve God, without my parents' knowledge, and you gave me an answer that satisfied me. But now having decided to serve God in my own country, and being freed from my former uncertainty, I come to ask your advice about the way of life I should choose, to serve God.' When he heard this, he sat down on a heap of stones, and I sat at his feet, and he asked me how I felt about it myself.

Here I must interrupt my story to add something which I should have said before. While I was waiting for Brother Klaus to return home I went to see Brother Ulrich whom I trust as a special Friend of God, and I explained my case to him – how I inclined above all to the life of a hermit, how I had long been burdened with anxiety and how I had now decided to make no final change until I had got together enough money to build a hut with a small garden and to provide for my bodily needs. He replied that he approved of all I had told him, and with my mind made up I left him. But now comes the remarkable thing. When Brother Klaus asked me what I

49

myself thought, the speech I'd prepared stuck in my throat and I couldn't utter a word of all the things I'd weighed up for so long in my mind, and agreed with the other brother, and I replied to his question by suggesting either the Carthusians or the Franciscans, that is the 'Brothers of the Girdle'.[1] What can I conclude from this, but that in his presence I was prevented by God from saying something that would not have been right for me? Brother Klaus replied that he was in sympathy with the Order of Minderbruder in Basel, 'But I,' he said 'couldn't follow their way because of their mobility, that is, because they are sent from place to place.' I concluded from this that the Order of Carthusians appealed to him more, because they remained in one place. So I asked him if it was not a disadvantage that the Carthusians held their possessions in common? He replied, 'Whatever Order you belong to, you have to live on charity. But if the possessions the Carthusians already have from charity are sufficient they don't need to go begging any more.' With this answer my doubts were set at rest.

Then I asked him another question. 'In what way should a man contemplate Christ's passion? Should he imagine the suffering Christ actually present before his eyes and suffer with him, as if it were his brother, or should he think of the passion as something in the past, in the sense that Christ has already overcome it all and reigns in glory, and rejoice with him that now all is well and all those tortures are over?' He replied, 'Whichever way you follow is good.' And he added, 'For God can make a man's contemplation as delightful as going to a dance, or just the opposite, it's as if he were fighting a battle.' When he spoke of dancing, I looked at him as if I were a little shocked that a man like him should talk of dancing. He immediately noticed this and repeated the expression: 'Ja, als solt er an ain dantz gon.'

Then I complained to him of my weakness, my failure to persist in the good life, how I did not stick to my good resolution but at the very first opportunity my desire would turn once more to the forbidden thing, so that I would be separated from God, as before. He replied that one had to rise up again quickly. To my shame, I have to confess that when I was talking to him about my way of life I said something more or less by chance which might have sounded like boasting, whereupon he, recognising the passion for righteousness which lay behind my words, said 'You should not boast of anything good in youself'.

I have written down these few things, from many, as well as I could recollect them, keeping to the sense, not the words.

THEOLOGICAL DIALOGUE: THE ANONYMOUS PILGRIM

The Pilgertraktat (Pilgrim's tractate or treatise) is the earliest printed work in which Brother Klaus is named. The author is anonymous – he just describes himself as a 'respectable pilgrim'. His visit to Brother Klaus probably took place between 1469 and 1477, but the little book appeared at least 10 years later, in three editions all published 1487-88, one in Augsburg and two in Nurnberg. The Augsburg edition, though undated, is believed to the the oldest, possibly published before Brother Klaus's death.

[1] The 'Brothers of the Girdle' (Gürtelherren) were members of an independent religious movement who followed a strict discipline of prayer and mortification. Some Franciscans and/or Carthusians may have overlapped with them.

The fact that the book was based on a visit to Brother Klaus is not in doubt, but the major part of it reports the Pilgrim's ideas rather than those of Brother Klaus. The author frequently records, however, that Brother Klaus agreed with him, in one case 'open-mouthed'. Because of the small proportion of the text directly quoting Brother Klaus, and the erudite theological speculations, which have little appeal to the ordinary reader, the 21 page booklet is often given short shrift in modern reprints of Brother Klaus material. Nevertheless, a persevering study of the quaint text conjures up an endearing picture of the two holy men struggling with abstruse problems. The only section devoted entirely to Brother Klaus's ideas, in which he explains what he understands by the wheel symbol, suggests that he was indeed personally interested in the kind of topics raised by his visitor, and had meditated upon them. The 15th century German lends a certain magic to the narrative which of course is lost in translation.

In Part One of the Traktat, *the Pilgrim arranges his material in the form of numbered questions. Before dealing with the first question – the love of God – he introduces himself:*

Once I was staying in a foreign land and visiting holy places of mercy and pardon, I met a man named Brother Klaus. When I looked at him, my heart rejoiced, because I saw in him a miracle of God – for he lived without natural food. I greeted him and he welcomed me kindly. Then I said, 'Dear Father, I should like to talk to you about the love of God. For Christ said: "Where two of you are gathered in my name, there am I in the midst of you. And I should like the Lord to be in our midst." ' He replied, 'Well, tell me what you know of the love of God.'

After the Pilgrim had explained what the love of God meant to him, Brother Klaus looked at me and praised me with a name I certainly did not deserve, being well aware of the gravity of my sins.

The Pilgrim's second question was about the Virgin Mary. He said he had heard how greatly Brother Klaus loved the 'noble Queen and Virgin, Maria,' and expounded his own ideas about the immaculate conception. He does not record any answer from Brother Klaus, except that his words gave the hermit great joy.

Then I said that if he didn't mind I should like to discuss something else. He answered, 'Speak!' So I continued, 'When we ask God for our daily bread, what is this bread?' He replied, 'You speak first!'

They went on to discuss the difference between natural or earthly bread, available to all God's creatures, and the sacramental bread, and the Pilgrim gives the last word to Brother Klaus:

'Then almighty God mysteriously enters the tiny Host and this is transformed, so that henceforth it is no longer earthly bread, but flesh and blood, with unspeakable grace, true God and true man, invisible. And in every Host that has been blessed by the priest, the Godhead abides, whole and complete. Here you have my interpretation.'

With the fourth question – the symbol of the wheel – for the first time the Pilgrim gives the initiative to Brother Klaus:

Next Brother Klaus said, 'If you don't mind I'd like to show you my "book" which I am studying, seeking to understand its teaching.' Then he produced a drawing of a diagram like a wheel with six spokes, as shown here:

He went on to say, 'Do you see this figure? This is the Divine Being. The centre represents the undivided Godhead, in which all the saints rejoice. The three pointed ends entering the inner ring represent the three Persons. They have proceeded from the single Godhead and embraced Heaven and the whole world. Here – they go outwards in divine power and here they return and are one and undivided in eternal sovereignty. That is what this figure means.'

Brother Klaus developed his meditation on the wheel in relation to the Visitation of Mary by the Holy Ghost, the Eucharist and the way to Eternity.

Of the Eucharist he said:

'Now see this spoke, which likewise is broad at the central ring and narrow at the outer ring – in this way the great power of the almighty God is contained in the tiny substance of the Host.'

Of the way to Eternity:

'Now observe this spoke also – this too is broad at the centre and narrow towards the outer ring. It represents the value of our life, which is altogether small and perishable. In the brief time (of our life on earth) through God's love we can gain unspeakable joy, which never comes to an end. That is the meaning of my wheel.' These words (writes the Pilgrim) rejoiced my heart. This was the speech he addressed to me.

Brother Klaus asked the Pilgrim what he thought about a visitation like the plague. Can a man escape this wrath? The Pilgrim said he would answer as well as he could. He quoted from the Book of Ezekiel, how a man clothed in linen and bearing an inkhorn (Ezekiel 9.2 ff) marked those who were to be spared because of their righteousness, and he (the Pilgrim) thought that those who are spared are spared according to God's will.

Brother Klaus looked at me open-mouthed. 'That is entirely my view – that no one can escape the wrath of God, but the man who remains in the truth and lives in the love of God – with him all will be well.'

The Pilgrim then expressed his conviction that the man who held fast to truth, had confidence in God and recognised that God himself is locked and secured in the noble queen, Maria, would never be overcome.

With some such words I took leave of him and asked him to pray for me and for all those who had advised this visit. He promised he would. And I should also pray for him. With this, he embraced me and said, 'God grant you health and happiness.'

The second part of the Traktat *is entitled 'The Pilgrim's Meditations' and it is not clear how much of it can be accepted as representing Brother Klaus's views. The author records that he devoted much thought and prayer to Brother Klaus's wheel symbol, and what its basic meaning could be.*

While I was thinking about it, I reproduced the wheel and made a picture-story for each spoke to help me to understand it.

To represent what Klaus had called the undivided Godhead at the centre, the Pilgrim says he decided to put a human countenance although he didn't fully understand it. He presented it in this way, since the Lord had said he would make man in his own image, but he adds that perhaps one might have attempted to represent divinity in some other way.

Six round pictures, or medallions, one for each spoke, represent the Creation, the Holy Spirit descending on Mary in the form of a dove, the Nativity, the arrest of Jesus in Gethsemane, the Crucifixion, and the sacrament of the Eurcharist. Five of the six pictures also contain small symbols representing one of the 'works of mercy' – to visit the sick, to welcome the stranger, to feed the hungry, to clothe the naked and to bury the dead. The sixth work of mercy has no extra symbol – the picture of Jesus being taken prisoner is reminder enough that prisoners should be cared for. The spokes of the wheel link the medallions with the eye, ear, mouth and cheeks of the divine head. In the four corners of the framework which encloses the whole design are the classical symbols representing the four evangelists.

The Pilgrim's special emphasis on the six 'works of mercy' is one of the clues which lead historians to think that he was possibly a Franciscan friar, or at least influenced by Franciscan ideas. Their inspiration was the passage in Matthew's gospel concluding that those who performed the humblest service to the least of their brethren had served Christ himself. In Matthew's list, the duty of burying the dead is not mentioned (Matthew 25. 31-46) but it was adopted later in Catholic tradition. The Pilgrim says that it was Brother Klaus who drew his attention to the connection between the sacrament of the Eucharist and the Christian's duty to give honourable burial to one who had partaken of the consecrated bread. This is the only reference to Brother Klaus in Part Two after the opening sentence introducing the wheel symbol.

The Pilgrim's account of the origin of the woodcut seems straightforward enough. He says he met Brother Klaus, discussed the wheel diagram with him and later prayed to God for grace to understand and use it for God's glory. As a result he designed the picture with the seven interlocking drawings which was made into a woodcut to illustrate his Traktat.

But there is a problem. In the parish church in Sachseln there exists to this day a painting in colour more or less corresponding in design and content to the Pilgrim's woodcuts, and this picture is judged to be older than the woodcuts. Durrer says as early as mid-15th century, several years before Brother Klaus became a hermit and started his fast, and therefore before the date of the Pilgrim's visit, since the fast is referred to in the Traktat.

Experts say that the woodcuts only seem earlier than the painting because the art of the woodcut was more primitive at that time than the art of painting with a brush.

In one form or another the elaborate picture came to be closely associated with Brother Klaus after his death and was a source of much speculation, and indeed controversy, at the time of the Reformation. For this reason its origin and how much Brother Klaus contributed to all the detail built up on the basis of the simple wheel diagram – his 'book' – is a matter of some interest. For the illiterate majority of those days this religious strip cartoon (for that is what in effect it is) had a great fascination, apart from the special significance of the face in the centre, the human likeness intended by the Pilgrim to represent God. This picture, previously called the Vision-Picture, because it was believed to be directly based on a vision experienced by Brother Klaus, is now known as the Meditation-Picture.

REMEMBERING STANS : DIEBOLD SCHILLING

Diebold Schilling of Lucerne, then aged 21, accompanied his father, Johannes Schilling, to the Diet of Stans, where the latter was the official scribe or recorder. He was thus an actual eyewitness of the event, but his account was written more than 25 years later as part of his general history of the period, the Luzerner Chronik.

After an introductory paragraph about Brother Klaus of Flüe, his leaving his wife and children to settle in The Ranft, his 22 years (sic) without bodily food and his gift of prophecy, Schilling continues:

At this time an upright and pious priest was in charge of the church at Stans, Herr Heini am Grund by name, a native of Lucerne, who was very dear to Brother Klaus in The Ranft. This Herr Heini knew enough to realise that nothing but war could result. He got up in the night and hastened to Brother Klaus and described the situation to him at such length that [meanwhile] the disputants were at their wits' end, and in the afternoon everyone was planning to go home and do his best to make ready, for no one could see any outcome but war. When they had eaten and were ready to depart Herr Heini came running from Brother Klaus, rushed everywhere into the inns and with tears in his eyes begged the deputies for the sake of God and Brother Klaus to assemble again and hear Brother Klaus's advice and opinion. This was done, but the message he brought was not made known to everyone, for Brother Klaus had forbidden Herr Heini to reveal it to anyone but the deputies. And so God granted the happy result; bad as it had been in the morning, through this message things became [so] much better [that] within an hour everything was settled and disposed of. My father, the late Johannes Schilling, who was clerk to my Lords of Lucerne (and with whom I myself had come to Stans as substitute) was immediately ordered to record in writing the agreement he had previously drafted, and this was then done as quickly as possible. Freiburg and Solothurn were included in this agreement, as they now still are, and the *Burgrecht* question was settled and a new document drawn up, called the 'Stans Report'. This caused universal rejoicing and was concluded on the eve of St. Thomas in the year 1481. The agreement was ratified with the seals of all the *Orte* (Cantons) and it was agreed to swear it with an eternal oath. The *Sempacherbrief* – how one should behave in war – was also confirmed and included.

PART THREE

The Other Dimension

THE LANDSCAPE IN BROTHER KLAUS'S HOMELAND presents dramatic contrasts which, Robert Durrer suggests, 'fostered in providential fashion his development as mystic and patriot.'

> Two worlds divide and unite on these slopes. From the rocky heights above Flüeli one sweeping downward glance takes in all the idyllic charm of the little country of Obwalden with its lush meadows and imposing farmsteads . . . Towards the mountains the picture is completely different. At the end of the plateau the ground drops steeply into the shadow of The Ranft gorge, where the dim light and the monotonous roar of the Melchaa efface all sense of time, and the old tale of the monk of Heisterbach, to whom a thousand years of contemplation were as one day, steals into the realm of the possible. But beyond that, the true alpine landscape begins; up there on the arid solitary mountainside, with its aura of legend and miracle, is the church of the Bishop of Myra, the namesake and patron saint of young Nicholas. One does not need to be mystically inclined to feel the psychological effect of this contrast, and to understand its influence on a man's inward development in the Middle Ages.

In spite of Durrer's evocative description of the scenery, it would be a mistake to think that the sunny meadows and orchards above Lake Sarnen symbolised an idyllic existence in contrast to a harsh and gloomy life in the narrow Melchaa valley. Klaus had experienced war – brutal hand-to-hand combat with pike and lance; he had sat on the bench with fellow magistrates who accepted bribes; he had led the resistance of the parish against paying tithes exacted for priestly services unperformed. There was nothing idyllic about all this. He resigned his offices, but could not escape the knowledge that such things existed in his own community as well as beyond it. The abandonment of his active life as farmer and citizen, the parting from his family and the physical removal from Flüeli to The Ranft, represent a dramatic outward break, but they do not correspond to a change-over from an idyllic life to one of gloom and struggle.

As we have seen, he had lived in 'two worlds' from his earliest childhood, and in both, joy and woe were woven fine. Toughness and sensitivity, practical sense and the vision of the dreamer, an awe-inspiring austerity and a gentle courtesy met in his nature. This contrast is well illustrated in the encounter with the troubled young man from Burgdorf, which has been described on pp. 49-50. The young man consulted Brother Klaus about a practical decision and a mystical one, and received help with both.

Today a well-maintained easily followed path leads from the car park at Flüeli to the little group of buildings at The Ranft. In case the pilgrim should hesitate, there is a signpost, and it tells you how long it takes: 10 minutes! It took Klaus 50 years, but not, of course, to cover the ground physically. An active boy would certainly have explored the place, fascinated by the rushing torrent leading to the awesome gorge. We also know from his son Hans that as a grown man his father frequently went there to pray when the rest of the family were asleep. But to exchange his family home in Flüeli for a lonely bare room – that was a very different matter. What led him to take this step?

The outward events of his life have been presented first, in an endeavour to convince the reader that Nicholas of Flüe, later Brother Klaus, was a real human being who actually lived. His homes can be seen, both the solid family house and the austere cell in The Ranft. He had friends who loved him. Some of his family disapproved of him (it is not difficult to understand why!); he was honoured during and after his lifetime, though his advice was frequently disregarded. Obviously the more spectacular events of his life cannot be imitated – becoming a hermit, the great fast, his peace-making achievement. But he himself would unquestionably have felt that these outward events were not the important ones, or rather that they were the inevitable consequence of his constant struggle to find and to do God's will. The division into 'outward' and 'inward' corresponds to no chronological development. His intense inward life existed from the beginning and when he became a hermit, intending to devote himself to a life of contemplation, 'the world' came to his door and was not rebuffed.

One of the strangest of his 'memories' was confided to his friend Heini am Grund who relates that Brother Klaus had told him that

> In his mother's womb, before he was born, he had seen a star in the sky that shone over the whole world and since he had lived in The Ranft he had constantly seen a star like it in the sky, so that he firmly believed that this star was himself . . . Brother Klaus also told him that before his birth . . . he saw a great stone, which meant the steadiness and constancy with which he should persevere. And at the same time, in his mother's womb, he saw the Holy Oil . . .'

(For whole passage see Part Two)

The Jungian psychologist, M.-L. von Franz, thinks that perhaps Brother Klaus had a dream which made such an impression on his mind that he came to accept it as a real event.

His childhood friend, Erny Anderhalden testified that

> Brother Klaus told him that when he was 16 years old he had seen a beautiful high tower in the place where the hermitage and chapel now stand.

Klaus's earliest visions were either intimations that he had a special path to follow, or reminders that he was in danger of losing the way. The most memorable of these warnings is recorded by Wölflin:

> One day, when he went to the pasture to see his cattle, he sat down on the ground and began as was his way to pray in the depths of his being and to give himself up to divine contemplation. Suddenly he saw coming from his own mouth a white lily of wondrous scent which went up towards heaven. But just then his cattle (from whose yield he supported the whole family) came past.

For a moment he looked away, fastening his gaze on one horse that was the finest of them all. Then he saw the lily bend down over his horse and get completely eaten up by the animal as it passed. Taught by this vision, he recognised that the treasure that is to be kept back for heaven cannot be found by those thirsting for earthly possessions, and that the gifts of heaven, if they are mingled with the cares and interests of this earthly life, will be choked just like the seed of the word of God that sprang up among thorns.

Wölflin describes another occasion (also mentioned briefly by Klaus's son Walter) when God spoke to him out of a cloud saying that he was a 'foolish man' if he thought that in his own strength, and unwillingly, he could submit to God's will, for willing obedience was what God wanted.

Warned by this voice he began to disregard the domestic interests over which until now he had taken such great pains, and instead to devote himself with more care than ever to heavenly matters.

This must have happened not long before the break.

The incident of seeing the little town of Liestal all lit up in flames and the psychic experiences the following night which caused him to return to Obwalden and to cease to take food, also seem to belong to this category of warning or guidance.

But he also had visions of a different kind. One of these first came to light in 1928 in the library of a Capucin monastery in Lucerne. It was bound up with different and longer versions of two others already described by Wölflin. The newly discovered texts were reviewed at some length by C. G. Jung, who had always been interested in his 15th century compatriot – 'my brother' Klaus as he called him.

These narrative visions are related in a naive, primitive style, which suggests that they may be the direct words of the hermit himself, perhaps recorded by Brother Ulrich. There are only two rather oblique references to Brother Klaus by name, otherwise the narrator is a 'Mensch'[1], or simply 'he'. In the present translation an identifying description has been substituted where necessary to avoid confusion, but the name 'Brother Klaus' has not been used except where the narrator himself has used it. Otherwise the style of the original has been respected except for the omission of some of the 'ands'.

These visions repay sympathetic study. At first sight they seem childish and derivative – their appeal reveals itself only gradually. The 'Singing Pilgrim' is perhaps the most vividly described and moving. The newly discovered 'heavenly quaternity' was the one singled out for particular attention by Jung. The texts are here reproduced in the Caspar am Buel version.[2]

Vision One: The Singing Pilgrim

It seemed to him in his spirit there came a man dressed in pilgrim fashion. He carried a staff in his hand, he had tied his hat on with the brim rolled back, like one who is about to take to the road, and he was wearing a cloak. And he recognised in his spirit that the traveller came from the sunrise, or from far away. Although he did not say so, he came from the region where the sun rises in summer. And when the traveller came up to the man he stood before him and sang these words: Alleluja.

[1] *Mensch*. Our language unfortunately has no equivalent word for a human being of either sex.
[2] Caspar am Buel was the scribe who had signed his name at the end of the Mss discovered in 1928.

And when he began to sing his voice resounded, and everything between heaven and earth rang in sympathy as the small organ pipes support the big ones.

And he heard three perfect (complete) words issuing as from one source; they were then shut away again as if behind a lock with a very powerful spring. And after he had heard the three perfect words none of which had touched either of the others, he still wanted to talk only of one.

And when he had ended this song, he asked an alms of the man. And he (Brother Klaus) had a penny in his hand and he did not know from where it had come. And he (the traveller) took off his hat and received the penny in his hat. The giver (the man) had never before recognised what a great honour it was to receive alms in a hat. He wondered greatly who this traveller might be and whence he had come, and he (the traveller) said: I come from there, but would not tell anything more.

And the man stood before the traveller looking at him. And behold he was transformed and showed himself bareheaded and wearing a cloak that was blue or grey, and then he no longer saw the cloak, but such a splendid, well-formed man that he could not do anything but gaze upon him with undisguised joy and longing. His face was brown which gave him a noble charm. His eyes were black as a loadstone and his well-formed limbs were his special beauty. Though he was wearing clothes, they didn't prevent his limbs from being seen.

While the man was gazing so untiringly, the traveller turned his eyes on him. And then many great miracles took place: Mount Pilatus sank down into the ground and the whole world was open to him so that it seemed as if all the sins in the world were made known to him. And there appeared a great crowd of people, and behind the people the Truth appeared, but they all had their faces turned away from the Truth. And every one of them had a great growth on his heart, as big as two fists. And this growth was selfishness, which led the people so greatly astray that they could not bear the sight of the traveller any more than one can bear the heat of fiery flames, and in terrible fear they turned round and went back with great abuse and outrage. From far off he could see them disappearing. But the Truth behind their backs – that stayed there.

Then the traveller's face changed and became like the face of Christ on Veronica's veil, and the man felt a great longing to see more of him. And then he saw him again as he had seen him before, but now his clothes were transformed and he stood there clad in a bearskin, with jacket and hose. The bearskin was flecked with gold. But he could see quite well that it was a bearskin. This bearskin suited him so well that the man recognised it as specially lovely on him.

And as the traveller stood before him looking so splendid in his bearskin, the man realised that the traveller was going to take leave of him. He asked him: 'Whither goest thou?' He replied: 'I am going up into the country'. And more he would not say. And when he set off the man gazed contentedly after him. Then he saw that the bearskin he had on was shining, now more now less, like someone wielding a well-polished weapon, the gleaming of which one can see on the wall. And he thought there was something that was hidden from him.

And when the traveller had gone about four paces he turned round; he was wearing his hat again. He took it off and bowed to the man and took leave of him. Then the man was aware that there was such love in the traveller towards him that he was quite overwhelmed, for he knew that he did not deserve this love and this love was also in his own heart.

And he saw in his spirit that his face and his eyes and his whole body were as full of loving humility as a pot filled with honey till it cannot hold another drop. Then he saw the traveller no more. But he was so utterly satisfied by him that he desired nothing further from him. It seemed to him that the traveller had revealed everything to him that was in heaven and upon earth.

A Second Vision: The Fountain

A man broke off his sleep for the sake of God and his Passion. And he gave thanks to God for his Passion and his martyrdom. And God gave him the grace to find nourishment and joy in it. After which he laid himself down to rest, and it seemed to him in his sleep or in his spirit that he came to a place that was owned in common by a parish. And there he saw a crowd of people toiling hard, and they were also very poor. And he stood and looked at them and wondered very much that they had so much work and yet were so poor. Then on the right hand there appeared a well-built tabernacle-tent. He saw a door opening into it and he thought to himself: You must go into the tabernacle and see what is inside; you must go through that door straightaway. Then he came to a communal kitchen. And on the right hand he saw a staircase leading upwards, perhaps four steps. And he saw some people going up, but [only] a few. It seemed to him that their clothes were slightly sprinkled with white, and he saw a fountain flowing from the steps into a great trough and on into the kitchen; it was three-fold, flowing with wine, oil and honey. This fountain flowed as fast as a streak of lightning and with such a loud noise that the place resounded like an alphorn. And he thought: you must go up those steps and see where the source comes from. And he wondered greatly that the people were so poor and yet no one went in to draw from the source, which they could very well have done, since it was owned in common.

And he went up the steps and came into a great hall. And in the centre of the hall he saw a big four-cornered chest from which the spring was flowing. So he went to the chest and looked at it, and as he was walking towards it he sank down like one walking over marshy ground, so he lifted up his feet quickly and came to the chest. And he realised that anyone who did [not] lift his feet quickly would not reach the chest. It was fitted at the four corners with four great metal plates. The spring flowed away through a runnel and sounded so beautiful in the chest and in the runnel that he was full of wonder. The water was so clear that you could have seen a single human hair on the bottom. And however strongly the water flowed out of it, the chest still remained full to overflowing.

And he perceived in his spirit that however much flowed out, there would still be a generous supply and he saw it splashing out of every crack and he thought to himself: I will go out and see what the people are doing, [why they are] not coming in to draw from the spring when there is such super-abundance. So he went through the door and saw the people working hard and yet very poor. He watched what they were doing and saw one man standing there who had made a fence right across the middle of the open space. In the middle of the fence there was a wicket-gate which he was holding shut, saying: I won't let you in or out unless you give me a penny. He saw another man twirling a club in his hand who said: The idea is, you should give me a penny. He saw a piper who played to him and demanded a penny from him. He saw tailors, cobblers and every kind of craftsman all wanting money from him. And before they had completed their work they were so poor they had hardly earned a

59

penny. But he saw no one go in to draw from the fountain. While he was standing thus and looking at them, the place was changed into a wild steep hillside, like the place where Brother Klaus had his dwelling, and he perceived inwardly that this tabernacle was Brother Klaus.

A Third vision: The Heavenly Quaternity

A man broke off his sleep for the sake of God and his Passion, and he thanked God for his passion and maryrdom. And God gave him grace to find nourishment and joy in it. After that, he laid himself down to rest. And while his understanding was (as it were) bound in fetters, although he thought he had not yet fallen asleep, it seemed to him as if someone came in through the door and stood in the middle of the house and called him by his name in a strong clear voice and said: Come and see what your father is doing.

And it seemed to him as if he came swiftly to a beautiful tabernacle, in a great hall, just a bowshot away. He saw some people there, and the one who had called him was at his side and spoke on his behalf, as a friend at court would do. And although he [the messenger] was speaking for him, he [the narrator] could not see his outward form, nor did he wonder at this. And his spokesman said: This is he who lifted up and carried your son and came to his help in his anguish and need. Thank him for it and be grateful to him. Then there came walking through the palace a handsome majestic man with a shining face, wearing a white robe like a priest in his alb. He put both his arms round the man's shoulders and embraced him and thanked him with heartfelt love for aiding and helping his son in his need. And the man was inwardly stricken and terrified at this and felt himself very unworthy and said: I do not know that I have ever rendered a service to your son, except that I came here to see what you had shown. Then he left him and the man saw him no more.

And then a beautiful, majestic woman came walking through the palace, wearing a similar white robe. And he saw how well her newly washed garment became her. And she put both her arms round his shoulders and clasped him closely to her heart in overflowing love because he had so faithfully helped her son in his need. And the man was startled at this and said: I do not know that I have ever done your son a service, except that I came here to see what you were doing. Then she parted from him and he saw her no more.

Then he looked around him. There he saw the son sitting in a seat beside him, and he too was wearing a similar robe; it was sprinkled with red as if it had been sprinkled with a brush. And the son bowed to him and thanked him warmly for being such a great help to him in his need. Then he looked down at himself. And he saw that he too was wearing a white garment sprinkled with red like the son. He wondered greatly for he had not known before that he was wearing it. And all of a sudden he found himself in the place where he had lain down, not thinking that he had slept.

Amen.

Orate pro schripteren (sic!)
Casparus am Buel de
Under Walden usw.

In his monograph on the visions Jung writes:

... I am a good deal less sophisticated than the so-called educated public whose philosophical embarrassment is such that it sighs with relief when visions are equated with hallucinations, delusional ideas, mania and schizophrenia, or whatever else these morbid things may be called, and are reduced to the right denominator by some competent authority. Medically, I can find nothing wrong with Brother Klaus. I see him as a somewhat unusual but in no wise pathological person, a man after my own heart: My Brother Klaus. Rather remote, to be sure, at this distance of more than four hundred years, separated by culture and creed . . . yet [this does] not impede understanding of the essentials . . .

For what interests us here is not the historical personage, not the well-known figure at the Diet of Stans, but the 'Friend of God', who appeared but a few times on the world stage, yet lived a long life in the realms of the soul.

Commenting on the vision of the 'Heavenly Quaternity', Jung draws attention to the 'parallelism' of the 'handsome majestic man' and the 'beautiful majestic woman':

The androgynity of the divine ground is the characteristic of mystic experience . . . Man as son of the Heavenly Father and Heavenly Mother is an age-old conception which goes back to primitive times.

He also points out that in this vision, 'the blessed Brother Klaus is set on a par with the Son of God.' This is indeed a strange episode. Some of its roots must lie in the passage of ·Matthew (25.31-46) which Brother Klaus probably frequently meditated on. 'Anything you did for my brothers here, however humble, you did for me.' It is highly unlikely that Brother Klaus would have consciously set himself on a par with the Son of God; he probably regarded this dream-like experience in a naive, uncritical way, without self-analysis. In the Caspar Buel MSS Brother Klaus is mentioned by name only in the final sentence of the vision of the Fountain:

the placed was changed into a wild steep hillside, like the place where Brother Klaus had his dwelling, and he perceived that the tabernacle was Brother Klaus.

The vision of the Heavenly Quaternity does not name Brother Klaus anywhere. But as we have already seen his strong sense of a divine call did lead him to identify himself with symbols of high spiritual significance – the star and the oil in the pre-natal memory, the tower he saw when he was 16 years old.

One very stange vision belongs to a category on its own. According to Wölflin:

all those who came to [Brother Klaus] were overcome with terror at first sight of him. He himself gave as the reason that he had once seen an enormous blaze of light surrounding a human countenance, and at the sight of it his heart was shattered and he was seized with terror. Completely stunned, he instinctively turned his eyes away and fell to the ground. For this reason his own looks now appeared terrifying to other people.

A French priest and theologian, Charles de Bouelles (Bovillus) visited The Ranft in 1503, staying overnight with one of Klaus's sons (Hans or Walter). He was shown Klaus's cope and his cell. In a frequently quoted passage, Bovillus wrote to a friend of a vision that had appeared to Klaus . . .

one starlit night as he was given up to prayer and contemplation. He saw the image of a human head with a frightful expression, full of wrath and menace.

Jung deals at length with this experience:

Here we are in the midst of that ancient dilemma of how such visions are to be evaluated. I would suggest taking every genuine case at its face value. If it was an overwhelming experience for so worthy and shrewd a man as Brother Klaus then I do not hesitate to call it a true and veritable experience of God, even if it turns out to be not quite right dogmatically.

In his autobiographical *Memories, Dreams and Reflections*, published towards the end of his life, Jung reveals how he himself, when quite young, had a shattering vision which led him to believe that the nature of God embraced more than just benevolence and love. So Brother Klaus's vision of the Face of Wrath was of special interest to Jung. In accordance with the mental attitude of his age, Brother Klaus would undoubtedly have believed this vision to represent God himself, and since God, for him, signified the *summum bonum*, Jung concluded that

> such a vision must by its violent contrast have had a profound and shattering effect, whose assimilation into consciousness required years of the most strenuous spiritual effort.

After describing the 'subsequent elaboration' of this vision, Jung continues:

> The vision of light had occurred several times before in his life. Light means illumination: it is an illuminating idea which 'irrupts'. Using a very cautious formulation we could say that the underlying factor here is a considerable tension of psychic energy, evidently corresponding to some very important unconscious content. This content has an overpowering effect and holds the conscious mind spellbound. The tremendous power of the 'objective psyche' has been named 'demon' or God in all epochs with the sole exception of the present. We have become so bashful in matters of religion that we correctly say 'unconscious', because God has in fact become unconscious to us. This is what always happens when things are interpreted, explained or dogmatised until they become so encrusted with man-made images and words that they can no longer be seen. Something similar seems to have happened to Brother Klaus which is why the immediate experience burst upon him with appalling terror. Had his vision been as charming and edifying as the present picture in Sachseln, no such terror would ever have emanated from it.

In making this judgment, Jung is assuming that the face in the centre of the picture is to be identified with Brother Klaus's vision of the God of Wrath, and this had indeed become a well-established tradition, so that the picture in Sachseln was known for centuries as the Visionsbild (Vision-picture). Jung drew attention to the fact that the wheel design was a classical example of a 'mandala', that is, the age-old symbol found all over the world to express the healing and unifying element in the Godhead. The idea of God as a circle is found in the teachings of the 14th century mystic Henry Suso, who influenced the Friends of God. It may well be that the idea had reached Brother Klaus and that he somehow assimilated his terrifying experience with the much more abstract conception of the wheel with the six spokes which he called his 'book'. It is now generally accepted, however, that the 'Vision-Picture' (as it was formerly called) is not an artist's impression of a single vision based on a detailed description by Brother Klaus himself; on the other hand it is highly probable that Brother Klaus possessed a copy of the painting in his cell and that it had great significance for him.

The subject has been dealt with at some length because the Meditation-Picture (as it is now called) is still closely associated with Brother Klaus and is frequently reproduced. (See also Part Two, pp. 53-54.)

Like many other things connected with Brother Klaus, the picture is strange to modern eyes.

Marie-Luise von Franz, a Swiss Jungian analyst, has made a detailed study of all Brother Klaus's visions (*Die Visionen des Niklaus von Flüe*) which is of considerable interest even if the analysis is not accepted uncritically as the only possible interpretation. Klaus's two 20th century compatriots, C. G. Jung and M.-L. Franz, are particularly well qualified to relate his symbols to their roots in Germanic myth and legend as well as to universal archetypes.

These references to modern analysts are not made in order to diminish the importance of Brother Klaus's spiritual experiences, but to suggest that they should be taken seriously as the symbolic representation of profound truths which the saint spent his life meditating upon and seeking to assimilate. While accepting the imagery of his time, he seemed able to transcend it and to relate his intimations of eternity to his concrete experience of this world. It was the same gift, which when facing the problems of his own small Canton of Obwalden, had enabled him to see further afield, beyond parochial interests. His contemporaries were not mistaken in accepting all the aspects of his strange personality as parts of an integrated whole, essentially simple in spite of its apparent complexity.

PART FOUR

Brother Klaus Today

IN THE CENTURY FOLLOWING HIS DEATH Brother Klaus continued to exert an influence on both sides in religious and political conflicts arising from the Reformation and Counter-Reformation. Poems, plays and cartoons, many of them highly controversial, kept his memory alive.

> Even before the rift in the faith (Durrer notes) the Brother Klaus literature begins consciously to divide in two directions: into the tradition of the political and pacifist Brother Klaus, the wise prophet and mediator in his native land, and the hero of faith, the saint who renounced the world and lived without food, turned entirely to the Beyond, the miraculous witness to the mystery of the Eucharist.

Brother Klaus's visions were taken seriously by Catholics and Protestants alike, but interpreted in different ways; for instance Luther managed to discover an anti-papal message in the much-discussed picture of the face at the centre of a wheel. He maintained that the six spokes were swords emanating from the head of the triple-crowned pope. Since at that time the painting was thought to depict an actual vision described to the artist by Brother Klaus himself, its meaning was believed to be of great theological significance and an attempt was even made (unsuccessfully) to have it discussed at the Council of Trent.

In contrast to the veneration in which Brother Klaus was held in matters spiritual and theological, Catholics did not find it convenient at the time of the Counter-Reformation to follow his advice against the 'pensions' system (contracts to supply troops to neighbouring princes) and this enabled the Protestant Reformers to point with 'malicious glee' (says Durrer) to the inconsistency of the Catholic leaders.

The polarisation of attitudes to Brother Klaus was of course only a side-effect of the 'rift in the faith', which brought deep antagonisms and even armed conflict between the cantons, imperilling the very survival of the Confederation. The last of these was as late as 1847, when an alliance of Catholic cantons known as the Sonderbund (Separate League) was defeated by Confederate troops after a short campaign. In the following year a new federal constitution marked an important step in the development and consolidation of present-day Switzerland. A more unified system of government was adopted and Berne was chosen as the federal capital. Ten years later the Federal Government finally abolished the system of supplying troops for military service, with the exception of the papal guard, thus at last achieving what Brother Klaus had advocated so earnestly. With modifications in 1874, the 1848 constitution is still in force.

The tendency to invoke the authority of Brother Klaus has continued throughout the centuries, especially in connection with the Swiss policy of neutrality. His advice was quoted as an argument against joining the League of Nations after the First World War and the United Nations after the Second. Switzerland became a member of the League of Nations, but not of the United Nations, though supporting many of the associated cultural and humanitarian institutions.

By the end of the 19th century the facts and legends about Brother Klaus had become considerably confused. In his delightful travel book, *A Tramp Abroad*, Mark Twain describes a visit to Sachseln. After referring to Pontius Pilate whom legend connects with Mount Pilatus, he goes on:

> Presently we passed the place where a man of better odour was born. This was the children's friend Santa Klaus, or St. Nicholas. There are some unaccountable reputations in the world. This saint's is an instance. He has ranked for ages as the particular friend of children, yet it appears he was not much of a friend of his own. He had 10 of them, and when 50 years old he left them and sought out as dismal a refuge as possible and became a hermit in order that he might reflect upon pious themes without being disturbed by the joyous or other noises from the nursery, doubtless . . .
>
> His bones are kept in the church in a village (Sachseln) which we visited and are naturally held in great reverence. His portrait is common in the farmhouses of the region, but is believed by many to be but an indifferent likeness. During his hermit life, according to the legend, he partook of the bread and wine of the communion once a month, but all the rest of the month he fasted.

In his light-hearted way Mark Twain was a careful observer and recorder of what he saw and heard, and this account probably accurately reflects the beliefs about Brother Klaus generally current at the time, but several points are wrong. Brother Klaus did not become 'Saint Nicholas' until 1947; nor is he the origin of the Santa Klaus legend. The real Father Christmas, a somewhat legendary figure, is Nicholas, Bishop of Myra, who lived in Asia Minor in the fourth or fifth century. Nicholas of Flüe was probably named after him (as well as for his grandfather) and it is easy to understand how the two holy men became confused by the passing tourist.

It is thanks to the researches of Dr. Robert Durrer that it became possible for the first time to get a clear picture of the historical Nicholas as distinct from the legend. Durrer, a scholar and art historian who spent the whole of his life (except for a few student years) in his native Stans, produced an exhaustive collection of source material, published during and just after the First World War. He did not claim to be writing a biography, but his introduction is a minor classic, and his two large volumes of annotated sources form the basis of all subsequent writing about Brother Klaus.

In spite of his aim of separating fact from legend, Durrer did not underestimate the importance of legend:

> The significance of an historical personality does not lie simply in the facts as they really were, but even more in the portrait which later generations see, and in the way it affects them.

65

In particular, the life of a saint does not end with his death, often its real significance only begins then. And so the simplified and idealised image created by the legend actually becomes the historical profile.

This is particularly true in the case of Brother Klaus. Nevertheless, the availability of a wealth of 15th and 16th century documents has brought Brother Klaus to life as a real human being, not dependent on legend to make him interesting.

The proliferation of studies after the appearance of the 'Sources' is remarkable: not only biographies, but novels, plays, an oratorio (by Honeger and Denis de Rougemont), books for children and specialised studies – Brother Klaus and the Desert Fathers, Brother Klaus and the mystics of Switzerland, C. G. Jung and M.-L. von Franz on his visions, studies from the point of view of Rudolf Steiner, Klaus and his wife Dorothy, and so on.

The canonisation in 1947, and the 500th anniversary of the Covenant of Stans, stimulated further interest and increased the stream of pilgrims to the places associated with Brother Klaus.

Today in the centre of the village of Sachseln a larger-than-life statue of Brother Klaus faces the busy traffic on the road from Brünig to Lucerne. Behind him, at right angles to the main thoroughfare, a dual carriage-way is formed by a shallow rushing stream running down the middle of the road. The stream is confined by wide grassy banks set with trees and flowering shrubs, thus creating a worthy approach to the church where the saint's bones lie before the altar, encased in gold. The statue is arresting, the large baroque church impressive, and the setting altogether beautiful, but it has to be admitted that as a first introduction to Brother Klaus it does not always produce the effect intended, for the cult of saints, the church interior of black and white marble and the relics within, are not to everyone's taste. Few could fail to be moved by the hermit's cell and the simple little church at The Ranft, but Sachseln is better appreciated by those who already know something of the man and saint commemorated there. Then one can understand the significance of the plain brown robe under a glass case, and appreciate the reverent craftsmanship which fashioned the gold effigy, but this is not the place to begin – nor indeed to end.

The saint's grave remained in Sachseln in spite of a request made soon after his death by some hermits in the Melchaa valley to have it transferred to The Ranft. The parish priest at the time refused permission, for reasons not recorded. He can hardly have foreseen the invention of the railways, automobiles, package tours, banks and souvenir shops, but his decision was certainly providential. Thirteen-hundred pilgrims can be accommodated in the memorial church in Sachseln, and since 1976 the Brother Klaus Museum has provided an imaginatively-conceived and thought-provoking introduction to the saint. By this means some of the pressure is deflected from Flüeli and The Ranft. Flüeli, though accessible by car and posessing three hotels, remains relatively unspoilt on its orchard-studded plateau. In the centre of the small village the simple timber house where Brother Klaus was born, and the one he built for his young bride, have been preserved as far as possible in their original 15th century state. Within a few hundred yards of these an extraordinary peace prevails. The few sounds that reach the ear – cowbells, birdsong, the intermittent

'St. Niklaus' ecumenical chapel in Frauenfeld (1960)

voices of children at play, the striking of the hours from the chapel at Flüeli and across the valley from St. Niklausen – seem merely to punctuate the basic silence and stillness.

The Ranft can only be reached on foot. The path leads steeply down through meadow and forest to the hermitage by the Melchaa. The place is not much changed since Brother Klaus's day. The room where he spent the last 20 years of his life contains nothing but a narrow bench against one wall, a crucifix, the meditation picture and a stone for a pillow.

The lower chapel, built in 1501, and larger than the one attached to the hermitage, soon became and still remains a place of pilgrimage in times of crisis. In 1914 and again in 1939 thousands of pilgrims flocked there to pray for their country and for the world. A fresco based on a design by Robert Durrer shows Brother Klaus standing on a hilltop surrounded by symbols of peace – children dancing round an apple-tree, a man ploughing, angels flying protectively around the saint's head – while on the plain below skulls lie piled up in heaps. The inscription gives thanks for the preservation of Switzerland through Brother Klaus, whose prayers on behalf of his fellow countrymen spared them the death and destruction wrought by the First World War.

The wording of this inscription suggests a difference of attitude between Catholics and Protestants towards their national saint, arising from their different interpretations of the role of saints in general. Today, however, a good deal of cross-fertilisation is taking place and there is growing agreement about the significance of Brother Klaus in relation to current problems.

The phenomenon of the 20 years abstention from food and drink (even if water is excluded from the definition of drink) is hard to accept, but many Catholics do accept it and Catholic encyclopaedias record other more recent examples of what is technically called inedia, though none for as long as 20 years. Even C. G. Jung, a non-Catholic, did not dismiss the tradition as unworthy of serious consideration. Today, however, there is less insistence on this aspect of the Brother Klaus story as part of his essential image, although it is an essential part of the story that in his own day his miraculous fast was widely believed in all over Europe and the fame of it led him to be known as the 'living saint'.

Is he a living saint today? There is no doubt that many of the pilgrims who visit the places associated with him find help in illness and comfort in affliction. The staircase leading to the upper room of his dwelling is hung with votive offerings and expressions of gratitude. He continues to arouse in many people a warm affection and a sense of his active presence which is often something deeper and more attractive than a self-interested petition for personal benefits. Not all the cures were obtained at The Ranft or Sachseln nor were they limited to practising Catholics. (See Appendix II.)

All shrines dedicated to Catholic saints have miracles connected with them (it is indeed a condition for canonisation) and it is not the purpose of this book to investigate or analyse in detail the healings attributed to Brother Klaus. Whether one explains them theologically, psychologically or scientifically (or all three) they are certainly real enough to those who have received answers to their prayers.

The question remains: has he any significance in a more general way? Can any lessons be learnt from the miracle of Stans? At a certain moment the pilgrim who spends more than a few hours in the tranquillity of the idyllic plateau above Lake Sarnen is faced with a challenge. Is this just a pleasant interlude, a refreshing holiday, an interesting experience, or has this extraordinary 15th century hermit-farmer any message for our angst-ridden age?

In his role as peace-maker and mediator Brother Klaus manifestly stood outside the conflicting interests of the warring parties. He had given up every earthly comfort – family life, worldly status and even ordinary everyday food (this seems to be the message of his fast, whatever its exact nature). His disinterestedness was clear to everyone and also his grasp of the problems to be solved. In the last resort it was his example and his authority that brought the contending parties to the point where the determination to make peace became the over-riding principle and transformed the atmosphere. Obstacles hitherto regarded as insuperable were seen in a different perspective.

Over the centuries the belief has become current that the mysterious and unrecorded message that Father am Grund brought to Stans from Brother Klaus included his advice concerning neutrality. This has more substance than appears at first sight. The specific points in dispute did not relate to neutrality as it is normally understood, for they were purely internal matters: the division of the Burgundy booty, the admission of Fribourg and Solothurn, the question of law and order, particularly as it affected inter-cantonal relationships. A more careful analysis discovers that what the Swiss call 'creative neutrality' is something more than just a policy of keeping clear of foreign entanglements and quarrels.

In *Waging Peace* William Lloyd, an American student of the Swiss phenomenon, traces the growth of the Confederation from its beginnings and analyses the means whereby it succeeded in holding the disparate elements together. From the time of the admission of Fribourg and Solothurn, newly-joined members of the Confederation were obliged to pledge themselves not to take sides in inter-cantonal disputes and to act as mediators if required. From this point of view the idea of neutrality is implicit in the Covenant of Stans and is an attempt to give substance to Brother Klaus's insistence that 'Peace is always with God.' In practice, neutrality can degenerate into a selfish desire to keep out of trouble, but it can be interpreted as a creative principle, the precondition of effective peace-making.

The Canton of Unterwalden (in population the second smallest in Switzerland) is politically and socially conservative, and there has been a tendency for fellow-countrymen in the centres of industry and finance to regard it as a backwater. It has no university, no important industry, only one well-known tourist centre (Engelberg). To counteract this, some cynics say, the Obwaldners have invented the Brother Klaus industry, and blown up out of all proportion the importance of their local saint. Now there are signs of a reaction against this disdainful attitude. Perhaps the traditions preserved in the heartland of Switzerland are not so benighted after all. Brother Klaus stands for a radically different scale of values, and jolts people into questioning the purposes of life. Is material success the only yardstick? What do men and women really need? What is the meaning of true simplicity? What does love of country demand of its citizens? Are there higher loyalties? No one accuses a man of deserting his family if he leaves them to defend his homeland. Nicholas of Flüe was aware, in a way that most men are not aware, of another world to which his ultimate loyalty was pledged, a mysterious world which he spent his life exploring and making real to others. The purpose of this exploration was not to run away from the realities of life on earth but rather to show them in a new light, to bring humankind a step nearer the fulfilment of the common prayer of Christians all over the world and indeed of all men in their own cultural idiom: Thy Kingdom come on earth as it is in heaven.

There is no tradition that Brother Klaus expected everyone literally to follow his example, to forego family life and exist without food in a primitive shack. His advice was rooted in common sense and stemmed from reflection on the practical problems of everyday life and human relationships as well as from the contemplation which leaves earthly things behind. Illiteracy in the Middle Ages was not necessarily a sign of lack of intelligence – 'this mechanical facility [literacy] is not as important as the accepted wisdom of the schoolmaster imagines.'

Within himself Brother Klaus possessed a compass which unerringly sought the true direction, and showed when to compromise and when to stand firm. This inward compass led him into the world of eternal values which to him was so real, and back again into the earthly country where most of his fellow men and women spent their lives. There was no contradiction in this – the things he perceived with his inward eye and with his physical sight were parts of one coherent whole. This undivided man has a message for our divided world.

APPENDIX I

'Switzerland'

IN THE 15TH CENTURY THERE was no Switzerland as we know it today and the term 'Canton' was not in general use before the 17th century. In this book the words 'Switzerland', 'Swiss' and 'Canton' have been used rather loosely, to avoid circumlocutions.

Dates of joining the Confederation:

1291 (total 3). Uri, Schwyz, Unterwalden (Nidwalden with Obwalden).

By 1353 (total 8). Luzern (1332), Zürich (1351), Glarus (1352), Zug (1352), Berne (1353).

1481 (Accord of Stans) (total 10). Freiburg, Solothurn.

By 1513 the 13 'Original Cantons', including Basel (1501), Schaffhausen (1501), Appenzell (1513).

The present total (23) was completed as follows:

1803 – St. Gallen, Graubunden, Aargau, Thurgau, Tessin, Vaud.

1815 – Valais, Neuchatel, Geneva.

1978 – Jura (formerly part of Berne).

1477 – *Burgrecht:* Equality of rights and support between certain city states (cf. the struggle to unite the European states).

Some 20th Century
Experiences of Healing

A NUMBER OF CASES OF HEALING associated with Brother Klaus have been recorded in the 20th century. The story of Anna Melchior of Klagenfurt in Austria is of particular interest. At the age of 45 she had been bed-ridden for 12 years with tuberculosis of the spine, subsidiary infections and painful complications. A Swiss woman resident in Klagenfurt gave her a picture of Brother Klaus and a book about him containing some of his prayers and a short account of his life. This introduction to Brother Klaus made a deep impression on her. She did not pray for specific favours but found comfort and strength in an inward communion with him.

In May 1947 she was so ill that the end seemed imminent; she was quite ready to die, thankful that this would relieve the strain on her ageing mother who had been nursing her at home for the past 10 years. Her sudden and total recovery took place after she chanced to see the headlines in a Catholic paper which her mother had put down on her bed: 'The Pope has elevated the Swiss farmer Nicholas von Flüe to the honour of sainthood.' After reading this Anna lifted her one good arm, with an effort, to stroke the picture of Brother Klaus which hung near her bed, and said: 'Saint Brother Klaus, I congratulate you.' She later described the experience which followed as an extraordinary sensation like an electric current coursing through every limb. She threw off the bedclothes, jumped out of bed and started to walk out of the room just as she was, in her nightgown. Her mother and two visitors had just arrived and the first words Anna took in were the shocked exclamation: 'You'll catch cold!' from one of the three astonished women.

It was 15th May, 1947, the date of the canonisation ceremony in Rome. Anna Melchior was completely cured and lived a normal active life for many years. At the time of the cure she was at home in Klagenfurt and had never been to Switzerland, but she subsequently paid a visit of several weeks to Sachseln as the guest of Ida Lüthold-Minder, author of the two booklets on which this summary is based. (See bibliography below.)

The story suggests that in Anna's case it was her courtesy and selflessness that wrought the miracle, not any direct petition.

Non-Catholics have also fallen under the spell of Brother Klaus. In Frauenfeld in the north of Switzerland an ecumenical chapel is dedicated to him which came into existence through the initiative of a Protestant woman who after many years of illness and acute anxiety found health and peace of mind in the church at Sachseln. Grateful for her cure she visited Sachseln regularly for many years and the conviction grew in her mind that Brother Klaus wanted her to build a chapel in his name. She raised the money by five years' strenuous effort, selling 300,000 cards each of which represented one building-stone. The attractive simple building, completed in 1960, is a focus for ecumenical prayer and worship, which is what she believed Brother Klaus required.

There are numerous other records of sick people who have found help through visiting one of the places associated with Brother Klaus, or just by meditating about him. They are not always cases of miraculous cures in the ordinary sense of the word. The present writer visiting The Ranft in 1983 met a German woman suffering from a congenital deformity (dwarfism) who had found peace of mind and an ability to 'live with' her affliction after visiting Brother Klaus, and now her annual visits give purpose and zest to her life. Such pilgrims tend to say 'visiting Brother Klaus' rather than 'visiting The Ranft', and everyone uses the name by which he has been known and loved for more than 500 years, rather than the more formal 'St. Nicholas'.

For details of cures, see:

Ida Lüthold-Minder: *Wunder und Verehrung.* Antonius Verlag, Solothurn, 1977.

Ida Lüthold-Minder: *Vom Himmel beglaubigt.* (Fuller details of Anna Melchior case) Christiana-Verlag 1972. 3rd edition 1981.

Gertrud Huber: *Begegnung mit Bruder Klaus.* (Origin of Frauenfeld Chapel). 31 p. pamphlet. c. 1962. No date or publisher. OP.

Marie McSwigan: *Athlete of Christ: St. Nicholas of Flüe.* Newman Press, Westminster, Maryland, USA. 1959. This very readable book unfortunately contains a number of small inaccuracies, but includes a vivid and well researched account of Brother Klaus's influence today, to which the present writer is indebted for introducing her to the subject.

Sources of
Quotations and References

Explanatory Notes

The existence of bibliographical notes is not indicated by footnote numbers in the main text, but the references can easily be picked up through the relevant page numbers given below.

The chief sources used in this book are from the collection by Dr. Robert Durrer entitled: *Bruder Klaus: Die ältesten Quellen über den seligen Nikolaus von Flüe sein Leben und seinen Einfluss.* 2 vols. 1,300 pp. First published 1917-21, 500 copies only. 1981, 1,000 copies printed in offset by Ehrli Druck AG. Obtainable from Staatskanzlei Obwalden, 6060 Sarnen, Switzerland. In page references below abbreviated to DU.

The most important documents in Durrer are available in a collection edited and introduced by Walter Nigg: Niklaus von Flüe *Berichte der Zeitgenossen.* Patmos Verlag, Dusseldorf, 1962. In this edition the 15th century German has been modernised. Abbreviated to NIGG.

The statements by E. Rohrer, E. Anderhalden, Heini am Grund, Oswald Isner, Hans von Flüe and Walter von Flüe (in this order) are from the Churchbook (Kirchenbuch), DU pp. 467-70 and NIGG pp. 123-131, here reproduced (with a few minor omissions) in Part Two (The Eyewitnesses). These witnesses are also quoted briefly throughout the book, in every case from the statements in the Churchbook, and the references are not repeated each time.

Where no other source is given, the relevant passages are from DU and can be found either in the detailed Table of Contents where every item is arranged in date order in Vol. I, or in the very full Index at the end of Vol. II.

Details of sources other than Durrer and Nigg are given below as they occur.

All the translations (except from the Collected Works of C. G. Jung, translated by R. F. C. Hull) are by the compiler of the present work.

Sources in the Introduction

ix   Mark Twain: see note to p. 65

ix   'Important turning point': P. A. Segesser: Sammlung Kl. Schriften. Bern: K. I. Wyss 1879. Vol. II, p. 1. (The authoritative work on the Covenant of Stans)

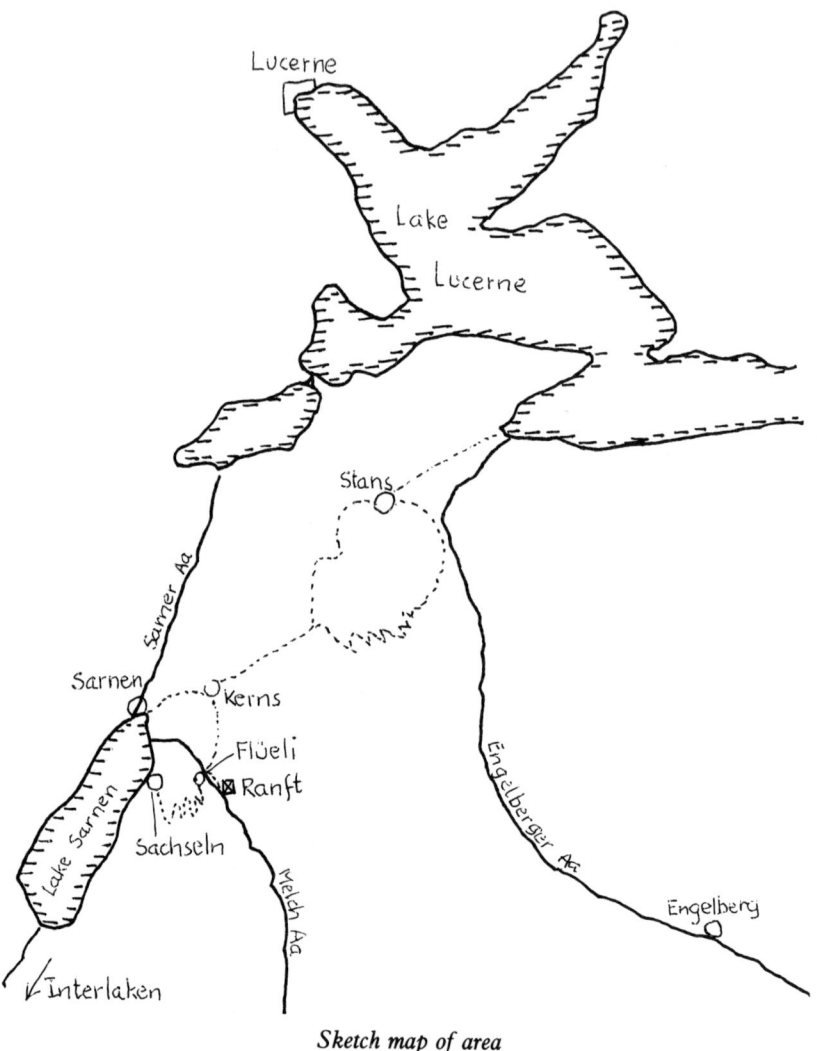

Lucerne

Lake
Lucerne

Stans

Sarner Aa

Sarnen

Kerns

Flüeli

Ranft

Lake Sarnen

Sachseln

Melch Aa

Engelberger Aa

Engelberg

Interlaken

Sketch map of area

INDEX